# *the* SPIRITUAL PRESCRIPTION

*for Transforming Relationships*

## THE ENLIGHTENED WAY TO LOVE, PEACE & CONNECTION

# MIKE BILES, M.A.

Three Peaks Publishing
Jackson, Wyoming

**LIMITS OF LIABILITY/DISCLAIMER OF WARRANTY**

Three Peaks Publishing
P.O. Box 2173
Jackson, WY 83001
www.thespiritualprescription.com

ISBN 978-0-9828329-0-5

# CONTENTS

# CHAPTER 1

# Wake Up to What Is Missing

*We grow up never questioning*
*that which is unquestioned by those around us.*

—Margaret Mead

*W*hat if nearly everything you have learned about love is wrong? What if the path you were told will lead you to happiness is only leading you further away from it? These are important questions you must ask yourself if your relationships aren't as fulfilling as you once imagined they would be.

"Keep your eyes on your own work because the person you are copying from may be a clueless idiot!" This is what my high school teacher said to the class as he caught me looking over at another student's test answers. In my youthful insecurity, I never considered that the person next to me or the people around me might not know what they were doing.

I had always assumed that everyone else somehow knew more answers than I did. My teacher's message woke me up from cheating in class, but I wish I had realized the more profound significance of his message earlier in my life. It took years, and I needed it spelled out for me.

If he had said, "Keep your eyes on your own life and relationships because the people you are copying from may be clueless idiots," now that might have been a lesson that could have had some real practical value for me down the road. But nobody talked to me much about relationships while I was growing up.

It wasn't until much later in life, after I had crashed a few, that I started to wake up to this fact. I had been copying answers to some of life's most important questions from people who really had no idea what they were doing.

When the romantic relationship model we grow up aspiring to emulate involves a prince, a princess, a wish-granting fairy god-mother, and a horse carriage that transforms into a pumpkin at midnight, we desperately need to take a closer look at the messages we're receiving and who's sending them to us. The Cinderella fairy tales we learn as kids are just the beginning of mountains of mis-information we're constantly exposed to in everyday life.

I don't know about you, but growing up, I didn't have any focused, formal relationship training or educational discussions about love. There wasn't a school in my neighborhood where wise sages, successful lovers, and happy couples gave lessons on rela-tionships.

For me, the only thing that came remotely close to it was an awkward 15-minute sex talk from my father about the birds and the bees. That was pretty much it for my formal education on love and relationships. The rest I had to pick up from watching my parents' and others' relationships, talking to friends, watching movies and soap operas, and listening to music. That's pretty much how most of us learn about love, and we should question the quality of that kind of education.

Well, I'm not going to ask you to take my word for it. I may be one of those who is clueless. Instead, I want you to know what is true for you through your own experiences; that is the best way to know for yourself what works. The Buddha said, "Believe nothing, no matter where you read it, or who said it, no matter if

I have said it, unless it agrees with your own reason and your own common sense."

The problem with our relationship education is that it takes time to be tested on our level of knowledge and skill. With something like swimming, you experience the evidence of your education right away—you get in the pool where the water is over your head, and you sink or swim. Either you learned properly and swam about, or you didn't and drowned. It's simple. The better trained and more experienced you are, the easier it is to glide through the water gracefully. If you never had swim lessons and had to rely on hope as your only skill, how well do you think you would have done?

People are lining up for marriage and throwing themselves into relationships with not much more than hope as their skill set, and hope is proving to not be enough. In research for this book, I interviewed hundreds of divorced individuals. Over 80% of the women said they intuitively knew deep inside themselves that they were making a mistake and that something was missing before they got married. However, they went ahead with their marriages, blindly believing they would be fulfilled.

When I asked, "What were you thinking would happen to make it all okay?", most of them said, "I hoped I would be happy and feel loved, and I thought it was what I was supposed to do."

You can't pretend to know how to swim when the water is over your head; there is no faking it, and you wouldn't rely on hope to keep you afloat. But you will do this with your relationships. And this is why you have to get real with yourself. So, how do you know if you got the proper training or have the skills that will prepare you for fulfilling relationships? Are you gliding with ease in your relationships, or are you struggling to breathe?

I assume you've been struggling some, or you wouldn't be here. You are definitely not the only one. Here's a look at how we're doing out there as a society:

- Over 25 million people are divorced. 5 million marry annually; 2.2 million divorce annually. (U.S. Census)

- 43% (2.1 million) of the 5 million marriages annually are second or third marriages. (U.S. Census)

- Over 150 million anti-depressant prescriptions are filled annually. (*Oprah Magazine*)

- 18 million adults are dependent on alcohol; 500,000 children under the age of 12 are dependent. (Alcoholics Anonymous)

- 19 million suffer from anxiety disorder. (Pfizer)

- 2.8 million children are neglected or abused annually. (U.S. Department of Health and Human Services)

- Over 60 million people are obese; 300,000 a year die of obesity-related causes. (National Center for Health Statistics)

By the looks of these statistics, it seems that many of us are drowning out there in the pool of unhappiness. The marriage statistics alone are convincing enough.

Aren't we all supposed to get married, stay married, and live happily ever after? That's what I had learned. That's what everyone seems to be attempting, but something is amiss!

For many generations, we've been conditioned to believe that marriage is the pinnacle of relationship success. It is practiced as a sacred union in different religions of the world and is a symbol of eternal love in our culture. It's a commitment that most vow to keep their entire lives, but it's obviously not working out as intended or agreed upon for the majority of people. The promise of lifelong love, happiness, and security that millions expect marriage will offer them doesn't seem to be guaranteed like many hope.

Those struggling to find happiness in their marriages often say, "Something is missing." Most people suffering from depression feel the same way. This "missing something" that many people feel, whether married or not, is the key to the door everyone wants to open.

There is a problem here, but it's not divorce or that we're depressed, overweight, addicted, or stressed out. It is something that all these have in common. These are the symptoms of an underlying spiritual disease. This disease has now grown to epidemic proportion, and it's highly contagious. Psychiatrist M. Scott Peck, M.D., wrote in his book *The Road Less Traveled*, "The absence of love is the major cause of mental illness" and "Patients are very confused as to the nature of love."

The real, often-unspoken and thus undiagnosed problem is that we don't know how to love ourselves or anyone else, and inside we're hurting deeply. We just don't know much about the nature of love; and because of that, we aren't experiencing enough of it. Much of what we have been taught is love is really nothing more than selfish need and physical desire; but we understand it to be love, and this is the problem.

We want love in our lives more than anything, and we're not getting it. We're not getting it in our marriages, and we're not getting it in our daily interactions. And we are getting unhealthier as a result.

The problem is not confined only to those seeking professional psychiatric or psychological help. Nearly all of us at some point are ignorant and confused about how to experience love.

We weren't properly educated about love, and most of us have not spent more than a few hours of our entire lives studying what the experience of love really is. Few of us know how to express our love effectively to others, we have an even more difficult time receiving it, and we're completely in the dark when it comes to loving ourselves.

However, we were taught to believe we know what we're doing even when we don't; and this is what has caused us to generate those atrocious statistics.

Not having enough love in your life is similar to your body suffering from malnutrition. You're starving, but on a psychic-spiritual level. It shows up as a non-specific anxiety (fear), a sense of inner discontent that claws and scratches its way to the surface. It's an inner discomfort that makes it hard to sit quietly with ourselves. There's a saying, "Your outer reality is a reflection of your inner experience." This would explain why 60 million obese people are eating like they're starving. When lacking the experience of love in your life, you will feel disconnected and empty. And being disconnected causes fear. And fear makes us desperate.

We want more, more, more of just about anything to stop the uncomfortable feeling, but nothing outside seems to satisfy this inner craving; nothing seems to stop the fear from coming up, at least not for very long. Although you may be ingesting things to fill your emotional belly and make the inner hunger go away temporarily, you know deep down it's not really working. No matter how desperately you try, you can't seem to be fulfilled. St. Mother Teresa said, "The hunger for love is much harder to feed than the hunger for bread."

Things like food, shopping, alcohol, relationships, drugs, sex, drama, work, TV, exercise, religion, meditation, remodeling the kitchen, and other activities can all be used to fill this inner void. For a moment. These are empty calories if they're distracting you from getting the real nutrition, the real connection your Soul desires to experience with others. You may be surviving, but surviving isn't enough for a full life. It's been my experience that nearly all of our relationship issues—as well as our mental, emotional, and even many physical ailments—are born from this one core deficiency, this lack of loving experiences.

In a 1945 study, Hungarian-born psychoanalyst Rene Spitz reported on orphan children who were raised in near-sterile institutions with little or no human contact. All of their physical needs were attended to; but the children received no affection, emotional support, or nurturing. Despite the near-germ-free environment, the children were very sickly. In some of these nurseries, more than 75% of the infants died. Spitz reported that a lack of caring, human interaction was fatal to infants (*A General Theory of Love* by Thomas Lewis).

This is a very sad, unfortunate way to discover the effects of improper care and socialization. It's also a very important discovery that we as a society can all learn from and hope not to repeat again. If a lack of love can cause the death of an infant, it can certainly make a full-grown adult sick.

If the pharmaceutical companies identified this lack of caring interaction as a diagnosable and treatable illness, they'd probably call it something like CDS, for connection deprivation syndrome, or LDD, for love deficiency disorder, and want to sell us a pill to fix the problem. Modern medicine, to its credit, has conquered many deadly diseases; but this illness that causes psychic pain has become the Black Plague of our time, and it's not likely to be cured with a pill. We are not chemically deficient. We are love-deficient, and this requires an entirely different kind of prescription.

## THE TRAIL OF TRADITION

– Author Unknown

*High in the Alps is small, ancient village. Every month some of the villagers must make an arduous 20-mile trek down the mountain to the city below to get supplies. At the trailhead lives an elderly widow woman who lost her husband to the north side trail many years ago.*

*One morning, Pablo, one of the village's strongest men, is preparing for the journey when the old widow stops him, as she does everyone, and says, "Pablo, the north trail is out. It is still covered with ice. Take the south trail; it will be much better for you."*

*Pablo replies, "The north trail is the one I always take. It's the one my father took, and my grandfather, and my grandfather's grandfather before him. And I will always take this trail." Later that day, Pablo falls on the ice and breaks his arm badly and has to return.*

*A month later, Pablo is at the trailhead again, and the widow stops him. "Pablo, the north trail has been damaged in a landslide. Take the south trail; it will be much better for you."*

*Pablo replies, "No one normal ever takes the south trail," and he heads off. Halfway down, he falls on the rocks, badly cuts his head, and nearly bleeds to death before he can make it to the hospital.*

*A month later, Pablo is at the trailhead, and again the widow says to him, "Pablo, the north trail has been flooded from the snow melt. Take the south trail; it will be much better for you.*

*Pablo mumbles quietly, "Yeah, yeah, yeah," ignores her, and walks on. When he attempts to cross the river, he is swept away in the icy, rushing water and nearly drowns. Fortunately, he is rescued and resuscitated by some men from the city.*

*A month later, Pablo walks past the widow, humbly smiles and waves, and steps on the south trail for the first time.*

It's been said that the definition of insanity is doing the same thing over and over again, always expecting a different result. This story is an example of what many of us do in our lives and our relationships.

We follow the path that we've learned, we get comfortable with it, and in time we discover that it's a dead-end for us with pain and emotional upset there every time we take it. Still, we keep doing what we know, believing, hoping it will one day work out; but it's not going to until we wake up and are willing to change our course. Instead of learning a different way, many of us would rather keep to the same course, keep failing, keep hurting and medicating away the pain instead of taking another path. But the pain or discomfort we feel emotionally is telling us something important—that we're not on our own true course.

There is a saying in prison and in rehab, "Your best thinking is what got you here." So if you are in a hole where you are not content in your relationships and at peace with your life, you are bumping up against the ceiling of your knowledge. You have peaked out.

What you've learned and believed up to this point isn't working to get you where you want to be, or you'd be there now, fulfilled and at peace. You need to learn and expand yourself! Are you willing to take a look at some of your beliefs? Are you ready to take another path?

## BELIEF INVENTORY

Your answers to the following quiz will create a general inventory of your beliefs about love and relationships. Go with your first impulse, and answer as honestly as possible. Move through the questions quickly, without taking time to analyze them.

On the line in front of each statement, write *Yes* if you now believe or have ever believed the statement to be true; write *No* if you do not believe it or never have.

_____ 1. When you're upset, it's usually because someone else has upset you.

_____ 2. There is one special someone or "The One" or a soul mate out there for everyone.

_____ 3. One day, you'll find someone who will make you happy.

_____ 4. Being able to control your life is an integral part of being happy.

_____ 5. Expressing sadness and crying is showing a weakness.

_____ 6. If you're with the right partner, he should be able to make you happy.

_____ 7. It's not really okay or admirable to be alone and single.

_____ 8. It takes a long time to really love someone.

_____ 9. A relationship's purpose is for the partners to make each other happy.

_____ 10. Sex and intimacy is the same thing.

_____ 11. You know you are in love when you know that you need the other person to feel happy.

_____ 12. The deeper you love, the greater is the potential for hurt.

_____ 13. A relationship should be going somewhere, progressing toward a common goal.

_____ 14. The more time you have in a relationship, the more important it is for you to stay with that person and try to work out difficulties.

_____ 15. Spiritual love is only truly found with the right romantic partner.

_____ 16. Once a relationship is over, it's best to stop loving your ex-partner.

_____ 17. It's hard to find someone to love.

_____ 18. You can't choose who you fall in love with; he mysteriously shows up.

_____ 19. A relationship breaking up means the relationship failed.

_____ 20. A good relationship will provide you with security.

_____ 21. There are certain crimes and actions that are unforgivable.

_____ 22. True love includes being able to feel what your partner feels—when he's happy, you're happy; when he's sad, you're sad.

_____ 23. If you're in a committed relationship, it's wrong to love anyone else.

_____ 24. A normal person in a normal relationship is happy all the time.

_____ 25. A relationship should be going somewhere.

_____ 26. Forgiving someone means what they did is now okay.

_____ 27. Your emotions always tell you the truth and what's right.

_____ 28. Fear and sadness are negative or bad emotions.

_____ 29. When someone really loves you, he should know how to make you happy.

_____ 30. It's important to save and hold on to your love for the right person.

_____ 31. You can't control your thoughts and emotions; they just come when they come.

_____ 32. When two people are in love, it means they are meant to be together.

_____ 33. The love you need to be happy comes from others loving you for who you are.

_____ 34. Heaven and hell are afterlife experiences: if you're good, you go to Heaven; if you're bad, hell.

_____ 35. If someone is really right for you, he'll be able to meet all your emotional needs.

**TOTALS:**    Yes _____    No _____

Any questions answered *Yes* illustrate an area of belief that aligns more with myth than truth. The *Yes*'s show areas where you've been conditioned to think a certain way; just because this is what is considered true by many, doesn't mean it is.

By the time you finish reading this book, you'll realize through much of your own experience that the myths you've subscribed to for so many years are actually keeping you from having what you really want.

## WE'RE POORLY TAUGHT BY THE POORLY TAUGHT

Generation after generation, our parents, teachers, clergy, friends, and media have kept alive myths about love and relationships.

This instruction has become deeply embedded in our psyches as truths. Some of the most common of these are in the preceding quiz, but there are probably hundreds more that are specific to our individual upbringings. The inherited beliefs about what love and happiness *should be* keep us from actually experiencing love and happiness in our lives.

We believe these myths and false messages because they've been passed to us by seemingly credible sources. Our parents, our friends, our clergy, and the media—referred to from now on as our teachers—all are sources of information we deem reliable. Where did they get their information, and how knowledgeable were their sources? They learned from their teachers and did what they did.

In 450 B.C., the Greek poet Euripedes said, "The gods visit the sins of the fathers upon the children." Over two thousand years later, this statement is still true; it's still happening. Our teachers have often passed along their mistakes and misinformation just as those did before them and their teachers before them.

The other day when I was watching a TV show, the show's psychologist was talking with a mother and her 20-something daughter who were both chronic shoplifters. The mother used to take her then-9-year-old daughter with her when she would steal. The daughter is now grown, has her own young children, and is now shoplifting with her children in tow; she has been caught several times.

The mother, now a grandmother, told the psychologist, "I never taught my daughter to shoplift. I never told her to do it. I never encouraged it!"

The psychologist about rolled over in disbelief at what the mother was saying. She may not have told her daughter to shoplift, but she sure taught it by example.

This is how it happens. Unconsciously, others have taught us, not only by what they say directly to us but by what they do and what they aspire to in their lives.

I was in a department store the other day, and a young girl, maybe 7 years old, was having a crying fit in front of a young, scared boy by a clothing rack. The mother yelled out, "Missy, you settle down. No one is ever going to want to marry you if you act like that!" This 7-year-old girl may now think about how her expression of emotion affects her ability to find a man to marry. Once again, this is how it happens. This is why this generational disease is so contagious.

And because right now it's all they know, those 2.8 million children who are victims of abuse and neglect every year will likely become perpetrators of abuse and neglect with their children unless they consciously seek another way, unless they learn something different. All the harmful behavior and messages they learned about love that got them injured will be passed on again. Unless they change now. And the same is true for you and me. We teach what we learn. We do what others have done, unless we change and learn a different way.

When we are children, we think our teachers know everything. They certainly know a lot more about how to survive than we do at a young age. Then, as we become teenagers, we start to think they don't know anything, and we experiment with life on our own to a degree. As we become adults, we hopefully begin to see clearly that they knew some things and didn't know others. This is the healthy passage from childhood to adulthood.

However, recognizing and accepting whenever our teachers didn't know something was often a hard pill to swallow. We have relied on them to take care of us, guide us, teach us, feed us, make our lives easy. We made them all-knowing superheroes of our lives at times. Because they also had the power to take away things, make life hard, yell, hit, control, neglect, abandon, we also made them super-villains. Whichever role we put them in, they had power that we didn't.

In a sense, as children, we made adults our gods with the ultimate power over us. So it's very contrary to our psychological system to accept they are just everyday human beings making mistakes and trying to make it through life as best they can. We've been conditioned to believe in them, believe they are always right; and we are oftentimes scared to contradict their authority, even when we know inside ourselves that they are wrong.

However, we must challenge their legacy if we are to find inner peace and inner reliance. We must learn to trust our own inner voice and our own experience over the myths no matter how ingrained those messages are.

The metaphor for this is represented in the story *The Wizard of Oz*. Dorothy, her dog Toto, Tin Man, Scarecrow, and Cowardly Lion are all seeking something they believe is missing in their lives. Dorothy wants to find home, the Tin Man wants a heart, the Scarecrow wants a brain, and the Cowardly Lion wants courage. On their journey down the Yellow Brick Road toward the unknown, everyone they meet along the way tells them The Great Oz is the Source for everything, that Oz has the power to give them whatever they need if the group will just "follow the Yellow Brick Road."

After a long journey with many trials, they arrive before The Great Oz and begin to bow to his image of magnificence. Toto runs off and pulls open a curtain, revealing a feeble little old man, and drags him out of hiding. It turns out that this little man behind the curtain runs the machine and the controls that make the image of Oz so awe-inspiring. The great, omniscient, powerful Oz is exposed for what it really is, just a common man, like everyone else. And he can't give them all the things they want for themselves because he doesn't have the power. They realize that they actually had all those things within themselves. They just weren't aware of them.

The Oz illusion of all-knowing greatness is also true for how we see the media—films, television, radio programs, and magazines.

The famous say it or show it, and we tend to believe it. They all have impressive, bigger-than-life images. Behind the glossy scenes, they are all everyday people with human wounds just like you and me.

You've got to pull these false idols of wisdom and power down from the pedestals you've given them and see what is truth from your own experiences. You've got to stop looking to others to tell you what to do and how to live your life. You have to start looking within yourself because that is where the real answers are to be found.

Seeing your teachers, big entertainment, the government, and media sources as fallible or vulnerable can be a scary thing. It means you now have the responsibility for making decisions and choices for yourself; it means you've got to take your life in your own hands. This is the difference between being a girl or a woman, a boy or a man. Just like Dorothy, Tin Man, Scarecrow, and Cowardly Lion, you've got to find home, heart, brains, and courage inside yourself because no one else outside can give that to you. You have to find your own way within you. And it is there.

In other words, "You've got to keep your eyes on your own work because the person you are copying from may be a clueless idiot!"

So how do you keep your eyes on your own work? How do you wake up to yourself? It begins by simply observing yourself, your life, and your experiences as they unfold. You do it by being conscious of what you've done, what you're doing, and what you intend to do in the future. If you can learn to trust your experiences over everything else, your relationships will transform because you'll know for yourself what works and what doesn't.

### CONNECTING TO YOUR EXPERIENCE

Much of what we learn in life is experienced only one-dimensionally. Reading how-to books such as this one generally gives you only a mental picture and mental understanding of a concept, which is only part of the whole picture. In order to know something more fully, you often have to broaden your experience of it. So let's do another brief exercise that will bring in some other aspects for consideration. Read the instructions all the way through before you begin.

First, take this book in both your hands and, with it still open, lift it to your nose, fan your face with it as fast as you possibly can, and smell the pages.

Stop! Okay, right about now, your mind has registered the potential event of fanning your face. It hasn't happened yet, so you only know the event according to your mind's image of it. You know it mentally.

Now fully experience it! Go ahead. Get the full experience. We can't move forward until you do it, so don't be shy. Go ahead. Fan the book across your face. I'll wait.

This brings you closer to understanding the four levels, or aspects, of human experience: mental, physical, emotional, and spiritual. In the preceding exercise with the book, at first you just had a mental experience. Now you may also have a physical and emotional experience. Let's take a look at these four levels and how to recognize them in your life.

**MENTAL** consists of the mind or brain processing data, forming and understanding thoughts, images, visualizations, etc. (Example: You visualized yourself holding the book and lifting it to your nose and smelling it; then your mind sent thought impulses to your body to carry out the process.)

**PHYSICAL** consists of perception through the five senses: smelling, touching, tasting, hearing, seeing. (Example: You felt the weight of the book in your hand, the touch of the air moving onto your face, and the smell of the pages.)

**EMOTIONAL** consists of thought-induced internal sensations or feelings such as sadness, anger, joy, shame, anxiety, etc. (Example: While lifting the book and fanning your face, the internal feeling/

sensation you felt was perhaps embarrassment because you thought it was a silly action; or maybe it was joy because you thought it was fun.)

SPIRITUAL consists of a deep sense of peace, love, blissfulness, connection, profound wellness, transcendence, unity with the Divine, oneness with a Force both inside and outside of the physical body, sometimes connected through what's called a sixth sense, intuition, or knowing. Spiritual experience has often been associated with creation or creativity or the source of inspiration and new ideas that come to us from beyond ourselves. (Example: Fanning your face with a book is not likely to drop you into the spiritual level of experience, but lovingly giving this book to a friend you care about could.)

The first three levels—mental, emotional, and physical for the sake of our focus and discussion now—are all part of our physical world perspective, the world we can observe, the tangible that we can identify with our five senses. These aspects are contained within our physical bodies and the observable world in which we live. The physical world has long been what Western world doctors and scientist have dealt with in their studies.

The spiritual world is the world beyond the known physical. It's the realm of religion, prayer, intention, meditation, God, Spirit, the Divine, and mystical events and experiences. This is an area that, until more recently in our culture, has been left alone by doctors and scientists; it was considered a whole different department left to the shamans, mystics, and religious clergy. For hundreds of years, an imaginary wall has separated the study of the physical and spiritual realms. And this power and experience of love has been a bit lost between the two.

Scientists weren't sure what to do with it, and the clergy weren't either. Now the wall of separation between these worlds is starting to collapse because the scientific community has been testing spiritual practices and their effects upon the physical world. What they are finding is astonishing to the scientific community but not so surprising to much of the spiritual community. A mountain of scientific evidence from research studies now demonstrates the effects of prayer, loving intention, and meditation practices on cancer, heart disease, psychological disorders, social behavior, and so on. So the physical world and the spiritual world are proving to *not* be separate realms as once believed.

Still, many of us live and relate to one another in only the physical realm, with little connection to our spiritual natures. And this is in fact what is causing us to feel like something isn't complete within us. A deeper, more complete experience is what many of us are missing in our relationships.

We've been conditioned to believe that the experience of love is something that can be obtained in the physical world, that it is something we can go out and find or earn like money, a job, or a new house. We think of it as an emotion that will arise magically. We search for love out in the world like we do a lost set of car keys in a parking lot. We want to be able to see it, touch it, hold it, own it, and control it; but love and real connection don't adhere to the laws of the known physical world.

Just because you marry someone or tell him you love him or he tells you, that doesn't mean the experience is there. If there isn't substance and loving energy behind the words, the experience is incomplete.

The real experience of connection drops you into the fourth, spiritual level of experience. This spiritual experience of love is what is missing and what we all need to feel complete. We just have to learn where and how to find it.

## CHAPTER 2

# Find the Relationship Within You

*God enters by a private door into every individual.*

—Ralph Waldo Emerson

*T*here is nothing more important to your life than your relationships because everything is a relationship. You are in a
relationship with your spouse, your friends, your family, your work,
life situations, and even with yourself. How you relate determines
how you experience your life. If you relate well to others and yourself, you will have a fulfilled and peaceful life. If you don't relate
well, life will be a painful struggle.

Most relationship experts and self-help books would have you
focus on improving your outer skills, like altering how you behave,
how you communicate, or how you get others to give you what you
want. Your physical, world-level interaction with another is only
a small part of any relationship. The real foundation of a relationship begins somewhere else. Contrary to what you may have been
taught, the roots of every relationship are deep inside of YOU.

How you hold others inside your heart determines the quality of
your relationship experiences. What's really important to your Soul
is how you experience someone from within your own being. One
of my teachers, Ron Hulnick from the University of Santa Monica,
often says, "A relationship is how you hold another inside yourself."

For some, this idea is a foreign concept; it's not what most of the world subscribes to, but this is why the world has so much difficulty with relationships. The world often likes to focus on treating the outer symptoms of problems and not the inner cause. But if you want to experience real love in your life, you have to dig deep inside yourself to find your spiritual core.

Many of us have been taught to look for God and spiritual connection up in the sky somewhere or through churches or in symbols and saints. We've been taught to look for love and affection from other people with the belief that only when they give us love will we be happy. In a sense, we've been taught to be lowly beggars seeking approval and handouts of love. But this is not how love works. No one or nothing outside you can give you the loving experience you ultimately need. It has to come from somewhere else.

Inside you is where everything of real substance is happening. Inside you is where you make the spiritual connection or lose it. Inside you is where the relationship with another blossoms or dies. It is from connecting to this inner Divinity that you are able to love unconditionally and feel deeply connected. Life can be Heaven or it can be hell. It all depends on how you experience the outside world from your inside world.

## THE HEAVEN AND HELL EXPERIENCE INSIDE YOU

Most of us have grown up in a religious culture that teaches us that Heaven and hell are places you go after you die. Three of the world's six largest religions—Christianity, Islam, and Judaism—combined make up approximately 52% of the world's population, or just over 3 billion followers, according to The U.S. Center for World Mission. Each of these religions has its particular version and teachings about Heaven and hell. What's common to all of them is the qualification for entry—death.

In general, these religions present Heaven and hell as places beyond this world of earth. Heaven is a wonderful place to look forward to some day. Hell is horrible, a place to be feared. If you're a good person by "God's standard" according to a group's particular religious opinion, you get to go to Heaven. If you're bad and violate that opinion and you sin, then you go to hell to be punished, for all eternity.

What about right now, while you are alive, here, on this earth? Jesus taught, "The kingdom of God is within you" (Luke 17:21) and "Whoever lives in love, lives in God and God in him" (1 John 4:16). Understanding how this view of Heaven and hell show up inside you is critical to your relationships. So let's explore this notion of Heaven and hell within you.

If you ask a woman who is passionately in love with someone how life is going, she would likely say, "I'm in Heaven!" If you ask that same question when the woman is going through a difficult divorce or suffering from depression, she'll probably say, "I'm going through hell!" You probably know people who've moved from Heaven to hell and then back and forth again in about the same amount of time it takes you to say "flash-in-the-pan romance." When love comes and goes with the wind, you will bounce in between Heaven and hell. Unfortunately, you will likely spend much more time in hell because there is no understanding of how you can remain in Heaven.

Heaven and hell can be states of consciousness that you experience right here in your daily life. You can experience Heaven or hell without ever getting out of bed in the morning, and many people do. You don't have to die or go somewhere; you just have to look within yourself and become aware of what's going on inside of you. Heaven or hell can be an inner experience, a perception. It's a way of relating from the inside out. Where you are depends on where your heart and mind are at any given moment. Your perception makes your reality, and being with love or being with fear determines your experience.

This simple story shows us how simple and easy the choice can be.

## HEAVEN AND HELL: THE REAL DIFFERENCE

—Author Unknown

*A man spoke with an angel about Heaven and hell, and the angel said to the man, "Come, I will show you hell."*

*They entered a room where a group of people sat around a huge pot of stew. Everyone was famished, desperate, and starving. Each held a spoon that reached the pot, but each spoon had a handle so much longer than their own arms that it could not be used to get the stew into their own mouths. The suffering was terrible.*

*"Come. Now I will show you Heaven," the angel said after awhile.*

*They entered another room, identical to the first—the pot of stew, the group of people, the same long-handled spoons. But here everyone was happy and well-nourished.*

*"I don't understand," said the man. "Why are they happy here, but they were miserable in the other room, and yet everything is the same?"*

*The angel smiled. "Ah, it is simple," he said. "Here they have learned to feed each other."*

If your mind is connected with love, you are going to be sharing love; you are going to be at peace and experiencing Heaven. If your mind is selfishly concerned, you will be afraid, you will be needy and in hell. If your mind is focused only on what you want at the expense of others, then you are in hell. If you focus on a loving connectedness and the wants of others as well as on your own, you arrive in Heaven.

I used to wake up with fear and dread of the day to come. At that time in my life, I woke up in hell nearly every morning. I didn't know I was in hell at the time because I had no reference point. I never knew Heaven by comparison; or it had been so long since I had experienced real love, peace, and connection, I had forgotten what it was like.

Some of us are living out our lives in hell, but we're staying so busy, distracted, and medicated that we aren't aware of it. We aren't aware that there is another way to go through life. We've become used to hell and know no other way to be or live. We've forgotten how to get back to Heaven.

## YOUR OWN VERSION OF HELL

Consider this, when you are afraid or upset, you are in hell. When you are angry or jealous, confused or frustrated, you are in hell.

If you have ever been in love with someone who dumped you and you felt rejected, you've spent some time in hell. If you have ever said or done something that hurt someone else and you felt guilty, you've been in hell. If you have ever feared not being able to pay your bills, you've been in hell. If you have ever made a mistake, regretted it, were embarrassed by it, or had a difficult time getting over it, you've been in hell. If you've ever been exposed to something horrifying and emotionally painful or had an anxiety attack, you know the darker reaches of hell. If you have unloving or judgmental thoughts about yourself or someone else, those thoughts are what put you in hell.

Hell is your inner experience of fear, and fear is what you experience in the absence of love. Fear and love are the canvases on which your life is painted. You can paint your life over fear, or you can paint your life over love. Either way, you will have a life. It is just a question of whether you will enjoy it.

Different cultures and different religions have their own mythologies and metaphors about the nature of Heaven and hell. In the Biblical story, God cast the angel Lucifer out of Heaven and into hell because Lucifer wanted to be God. In Lucifer's separation from God, Lucifer suffered great fear and deep pain because he was no longer in the aura that surrounded God; the angel was cut off from the Source that provided love and peace.

If you were Lucifer and you believed you were not going to ever be at peace or feel love again, that would be a terrifying, lost, desperate, hopeless experience. At times, many of us have been there and felt those things. And it creates a very dark, lonely, and painful existence. Perhaps nothing is more painful than feeling this separation.

Here's how it works from a practical standpoint. When you are experiencing a connection with someone, your Soul is able to experience the Soul in him. You feel bonded and peaceful; you feel love.

However, if you are in conflict with this person, a shift happens inside you. You no longer experience that Soul in them or yourself; you begin to feel this deep sense of fear, separateness. A disconnect from loving experience occurs inside you, and you move from Heaven into hell. The separation is what moves you into the experience of hell. Anytime you stop loving, you start fearing; and this puts you in hell.

Any conflict that arises with another is like the conflict between God and the angel Lucifer. One moment, both of you are in Heaven, together in Oneness, surrounded by love and peace. The next moment, after the conflict arises, you are both in hell, feeling separated and suffering.

You can observe this yourself. If during a nice, peaceful dinner together with loved ones someone brings up a religious, political, or greatly controversial topic, the Heavenly experience often transforms into a hellish one. People begin to get upset, defensive, and fight. The connection and peace they felt a moment ago disappears as they slide into disconnection and fear. The gathering hasn't changed; just the heartset and mindset of the people has changed. One moment, everyone is in the love/Heaven space; then next, they're all in the fear/hell space.

An event like this shows you that hell can be of your own making, something you create inside yourself. Oscar Wilde said, "We are each our own devil, and we make this world our hell." You can make hell show up within you right now. You can have a hellish relationship experience and not even move an inch or see anybody for a hundred miles. All you have to do is visualize a past situation that was very upsetting.

In doing this, your mind will experience it as if it happening right now. The more vivid the scene is in your mind, the more real it will seem. Your body doesn't recognize the difference between a vividly imagined thought and a real present-moment experience. So if you think of something that separates, frightens, or upsets you, you can move your inner experience to hell all by yourself.

It's this ability that is making the world sick in many different ways. It's this ability, better called a disability, that destroys relationships.

Of course, there are varying degrees and durations of hell. These can range from momentary embarrassment to lifelong, life-threatening depression and many things in between. How disapproving and conflicted you are with yourself, others, and the ways of the world will affect the intensity of your visit in hell.

This form of Hell is not an exclusive prison for bad people or sinners. We all have a cell reserved for us. Some of us just pass through from time to time on minor thought infractions while others have made it home. The decision is up to us how long and how intense our visits there will be.

You have a choice, called free will. You're free to experience your world in such a way that hell becomes your home, or you can choose to align with love and make Heaven your home.

## EGO—YOUR INNER LINK TO HELL

The part of your mind that lands you in hell is what many have called "The Ego."

Imagine your mind is like a computer with two internal, hard-drive storage discs. One of them is connected to the Soul in you. The other is programmed and set up by you, your parents, friends, lovers, schoolteachers, neighbors, priest, the government, the media, and whoever else has crossed your path since birth—this is your ego. One is pure truth and connected to the Soul. The other is part truth, part lies, part misinformation, and part others' egos.

The disc programmed by the Soul runs smoothly, perfectly, with no glitches. It is in sync with all things. The ego's disc is irrational, erratic, and full of static, distortion, and viruses.

The ego is simply man's version of the universe's reality. Man puts his own spin on reality at times because man often thinks he is the center of the universe. Man thinks that he is in charge.

Lucifer is the metaphor for what psychologists have come to call the ego. Man's ego thinks he can take over the role of God and believes he should be in charge. The ego tries to substitute superficial things to fill the inner emptiness left by not being spiritually connected. Because Lucifer (ego) can't get back to connection with God and love through his Soul, Lucifer seeks a substitute for spiritual connection. Lucifer is always seeking something to pacify his inner pain, but nothing will ever work because nothing can replace love that comes from connection to the Soul that is connected to something bigger than himself.

The ego is the part of you that tells you that you need more than what you've already been given by the universe. It tells you that you are inadequate as you are, that you are missing something and must get it from someone or somewhere else. This belief, this process will land you in hell every time, and you will stay there until you change this belief.

The ego is the voice behind every thought and every action that is not loving. It is the part of you that resides separate from your loving side. It's the aspect of you that sees you as separate from others, separate from nature, separate from the universe. It is the Lucifer aspect in you that chooses to move away from the God aspect in you.

The ego is your self-concerned human mind. It is the part concerned only with "my needs" and "my wants" that stem from your insecurities and feelings of being alone. Your ego aspect is selfish, vain, concerned with preserving its image and being right. It seeks security in things that cannot offer it real security. The ego is who you think you are until you realize you're a Soulful being connected to something much more profound.

Your ego wants you to think you are your job, your accomplishments, your reputation, your spouse, your money, your car, your status, and so on. It wants you to think of these as things that will bring you satisfaction and security. But they won't because they are only a substitute for what it really craves, which is love.

### What your ego may do to you during a normal day:

- Cause you to experience fear, guilt, upset.

- Point the finger of blame, and condemn others.

- Judge others as unworthy; judge yourself as unworthy.

- Tell you that you are not good enough and can't do it or have it.

- Have you think negatively of the past or future in order to frighten you.

■ Direct you to seek love and affirmation from other people or things.

■ Cause you to feel hate and the desire to attack.

■ Compare you to others physically, financially, materially, emotionally, etc.

■ Falsely direct you to pursue external sources for internal fulfillment (money, drugs, power, prestige, another person, career, material items, etc.).

■ Tell you love equals pain, and cause you to avoid intimacy.

■ Tell you that what others say negatively about you is true.

■ Try to convince you that you need someone or something to be at peace.

■ Cause you to defend your position or blame others for your inner troubles.

■ Tell you to avoid expressing and experiencing your emotions because that is a sign of weakness.

■ Tell you that change is dangerous and to be avoided.

The ego shows up and speaks to us in a million different ways; these are just a few. Throughout the book, we're going to talk much more about how the ego operates. If you want to test yourself to determine if you or someone else is living from the ego, ask yourself these questions: Are you making someone wrong? Is someone not good enough?

If the answer is *Yes,* the ego's voice is doing its dirty work on someone; and most often it's doing it to its host—YOU!

## WHAT IS HEAVEN?

A common vision of Heaven is a beautiful place in the clouds or sky where everyone is blissful and reunited with those they love. It's a place of peace, unity, and eternal happiness. It is a place where everyone is connected with you. That, translated into your inner experience, equates to love and inner peace.

Heaven is experienced through unconditional loving thoughts about yourself and others. It's simple. If you're thinking loving thoughts and you feel connected in heart, you're in Heaven.

If you've ever cried tears of joy from watching a touching scene in a movie, that was a moment in Heaven. If you've ever felt the warmth and joy come through your heart from helping someone in need, that was Heaven. If you've ever felt love for someone and could see nothing but beauty and perfection in the person, that was the Heavenly experience. If you've ever felt moved by witnessing someone's selfless act of heroism, or if you've had a deep sense of compassion for someone's suffering, that was Heaven. If you've ever experienced a sense of closeness, oneness, and wonder with nature—whether it be the awe of a beautiful sunset or the admiration of a wild animal, that is the inner experience of Heaven.

Many experiences can bring you to this place within yourself, and they all have one thing in common—loving connection. Loving connection is unconditional appreciation. When you experience this unconditional appreciation inside yourself, that is Heaven. And it doesn't matter to whom or what this love is directed—love for your pet, your mother, your spouse, your friend, the trees, the ocean, yourself—it doesn't matter.

If you don't think you're experiencing enough of this in your relationships, your unconditional appreciation is what's missing. If you have an unconditional appreciation in your mind and a warm, connecting tug of joy filling your heart, that is the experience of

Heaven within. And if you have this experience, you want for nothing else. This is the peak of all peak experiences.

Heaven is an inner joining with the Soulful Essence, whether it be with your own Essence within you or someone else's. Yours or theirs, it doesn't matter; when connected to a Soul, you can feel connected to all Souls.

When you have love for someone, you can't really show your inner experience to him; it's more of an unseen energy, a feeling of being joined to him by a mystical thread of inner experience. And one thing you've probably experienced is that the other person doesn't have to be in your presence for you to feel this connection.

You can experience it all by yourself, within yourself. You can be in California, and someone you love can be in New York. It doesn't matter; you still feel the inner presence and connection. Even if a loved one dies, you can still feel the connection inside yourself.

Love can have a very calming, centering effect on your entire being. Love may also be experienced with sadness. Love is not only experienced as a specific emotion but rather a screen or background state of being, behind the emotion. This is why Heaven has been described as a place beyond this world—the experience of Heaven takes us to a place that is not confined or defined by the physical laws of earth as we know them. This inner experience transcends and rises above the earthly, material plane. Soul-connected love knows no physical bounds.

Being in Heaven doesn't mean you are always blissfully happy and excited. That can be an emotional experience resulting from love; but there may be other, less emotionally dramatic responses. When you are experiencing Heaven, you will know it by this very important quality: You will not have a need to do, say, or change anything or anyone to make the situation different. It will all be perfectly beautiful just as it is.

## THE SOUL—YOUR INNER LINK TO HEAVEN

Emerson said, "To different minds, the same world is a hell and a Heaven." The world you live in, whether it be hell or Heaven, is determined by which one of your two mindsets you use to experience the world.

You've been taught that you must change the world around you to make it a better place. However, the world you must first change is the one inside you. In order to transform a world of hell into a world of Heaven, you have to switch on your loving mind and loving heart to the world.

And you are the only one who can make this switch happen. You can't wait or expect the world or those around you to adjust. You have to do it inside yourself. If you wait on the world to change, you'll wait forever.

If you can learn to use the aspect of your Soul's mind that is connected to the Spiritual Source within everyone, the world will change before your eyes. It happens when you shift your thoughts and reasons not to love out of your mind and bring thoughts and reasons to love into your mind. It's a subtle shift inside yourself, and you may have to practice to get to the experience.

On the following page is a list of words that may bring you closer to the experiences we've been discussing. Read all the words of the ego mindset column first. Let each word sink in to a level where you relate to the word's meaning. Check in with yourself. Become aware of how these words may affect your inner experience. Then read the Soul mindset list, and notice if there is a difference in how you feel inside.

Moving into a Soul-connected place happens by intention. Your intention, your desire to connect with the Soul will often be enough to make the shift. It's like climbing over a high fence. Sometimes, you have to put in some extra effort, and you have to push through the fear in order to get over the top rail. Getting to a

| WORDS ASSOCIATED WITH THE EGO MINDSET | WORDS ASSOCIATED WITH THE SOUL MINDSET |
|---|---|
| fear | peace |
| control | allow |
| should | may |
| antagonize | nurture |
| attachment | surrender |
| expectation | intention |
| reactive | accepting |
| resistant | experiential |
| closed | open |
| protective | vulnerable |
| scarcity | abundance |
| degrade | empower |
| fix | service |
| punish | correct |
| separation | connection |
| judgment | compassion |
| jealous | grateful |
| manipulating | asking |
| needy | appreciative |
| desperate | patient |
| dependent | interdependent |
| insistent | encouraging |
| evasive | available |
| insensitive | tolerant |
| rude | polite |
| wronging | forgiving |
| apathetic | caring |
| belittling | supporting |
| criticizing | praising |
| telling | listening |

loving state or expressing that love almost always requires pushing through some fear inside of you.

It's not always easy, if it were, everyone would always be in Heaven.

The Soulful mind is the Spirit's light in you; it's one in the same. This light is not only on inside you, it's on inside everyone. Much of the time you have a dark shade over this light, dimming its brilliance. This dark shade is your ego. So you may not be aware of your light because the ego has a way of smothering it.

Imagine a string of white lights like the ones used to decorate trees. On this string, there are trillions and trillions of bulbs—a bulb for each person, each creature, each atom in the universe—and we are all strung together, connected by this invisible electrical wire that the energy of love flows through. When your fear shades your own light, it tends to slow the flow of energy to the lights closest to you on the string, making your world darker around you.

When your light shines brightly, its brilliance tends to speed the flow of energy to those close to you; and your world around you becomes a brighter place.

If you have ever noticed or been around people who really love and support each other, the energy around them is radiant. Maybe you've seen a couple or some friends whose love is bigger than life for one another. Their shared love can change a room full of people. Their shared light can inspire and spread energy to the bulbs all around them.

Deep down, we all want to remove our shades. We all want to shine our light and share love. We've just been afraid to do it. We've been afraid our affections will be denied and unreturned. It's this fear of rejection that keeps us from experiencing Heaven.

The true light, the true love that comes through the Soul isn't afraid of being denied or rejected because it doesn't need the approval of others to shine. Unconditional love makes no demands on another, has no want from another. Unconditional love of the Soul is given freely and doesn't care how another responds. It needs no response, no affirmation, no approval, no return. It already has it from the Divine Source within, and this Source never changes Its mind. The Soul gives love without want or expectation because it is the natural thing to do.

The Soul's mission is to provide you with the experience of Heaven through unlimited, unconditional loving and peace. When you are connected to the Soul within, you will be at peace with yourself and others, no matter what the situation.

### What your Soul may do to you during a normal day:

- Cause you to experience peace, calm, joy, bliss.

- Remind you of your divine perfection and the divine perfection in others.

- Focus your attention on gratitude for what you have now.

- Direct you toward sharing and giving without conditions.

- Direct you to find peace through spiritual connection.

- Cause you to acknowledge the Loving Essence and Divine in all things.

- Tell you that all is well and just as it should be in this moment.

- Focus your attention and experience on the present moment.

- Support and allow others to be as they are, where they are.

- Find joy in giving to others in service of them.

- Inspire and relax you.

- Perceive the world free of judgment and in proper order.

- Act with thought, kindness, and loving intention.

- Have reverence for all things.

## GETTING TO HEAVEN

Arriving in Heaven is really a very simple thing to do. We just make it harder than it has to be. Because we're not totally committed to getting there, we shy away and retreat at the first sign of resistance. We want love in our lives, but we aren't willing to put in the effort to get there. We think love will just someday show up on our doorstep, wrapped up with a pretty red bow. We're taught that love finds us, but it doesn't.

If you're not used to being in Heaven, getting yourself there is going to take some unfamiliar action on your part.

Muhammad said, "A man's true wealth hereafter is the good he does in the world to his fellow man." Jesus said, "Love one another." The Buddha said, "Hatreds do not ever cease in this world by hating, but by love; this is an eternal truth." The world's most-followed spiritual teachers tell us to treat each other with love, kindness, and caring. This is what it takes to arrive in a Heavenly experience, but we often don't love all the way through. We extend a loving hand, and then we yank it back at the first sign of trouble.

To reach the experience of Heaven, you have to love; and that means 100%, no pulling back, no partial acceptance, no "I love you, but ____." It means you love without condition, without wanting something from another, with complete acceptance.

If you have lived much of your life in fear of being hurt, like I have, you've probably built up a lot of emotional defenses. There are hundreds of different ways to create walls between us and others. We build these walls to protect the wounded part inside of us. We think it's wise to protect ourselves from the pain that comes with love, but we're wrong. The irony is, the only way to heal that wounded part of us is by allowing more love to flow, not less.

Your personal walls are like the walls of a fortress and were built to protect a fragile child inside from the hostiles outside. Now those walls that keep others out are also keeping you in. Anything that protects you also keeps you imprisoned.

*The Course in Miracles* teaches, "In my defenselessness my safety lies." Which means, when you stop protecting yourself and pull down your barriers, you allow love to come in and go out freely. When you realize that you put yourself in Heaven and you put yourself in hell, you don't need to protect yourself from anyone else anymore. It's not "they" who are in charge or control of your state; it is you.

Heaven is found through connection. The problem is we continue to pursue situations that promise us happiness but really only disconnect us further.

Reaching Heaven is about seeing the world and everyone in it with soft eyes—eyes that can see past the false façades, the masks, and images others put out in front of us. It is about seeing the Divine inside others, treating them with dignity and kindness even when you don't want to be around them. It's about living from the Soul.

## CHAPTER 3

# Give Up the Fruitless, Endless Search

*It's not easy to find happiness in ourselves,*
*and it's not possible to find it elsewhere.*

—Agnes Repplier

Nearly every day, you're being sold happiness in one form or another.

Traditionally, little girls are sold the idea that one day they will meet Mr. Right who will make them happy; little boys are sold the idea that one day they'll be millionaire business owners or superstar professional athletes and will then be happy. Commercial advertising shows beautiful models and handsome actors glowingly happy because a particular product has suddenly changed their lives for the better.

The message? "Someday, you can be happy. Happiness is out there. You just have to get the right person, the right career, and enough money to buy the right stuff!" We've been surrounded and bombarded by messages telling us love and happiness are things we can obtain, own, or achieve. There are so many people trying to sell us, we've become numb and desensitized. The messages have become so popular and commonplace that we rarely question them; we just go along with them as if they were the truth.

Yet every day, we're duped by one of the oldest selling and propaganda techniques in the world. It's been used to push products and ideas by everyone, from everyday shampoo manufacturers to evil politicians like Adolph Hitler. This psychologically sophisticated sales approach is called Problem-Reaction-Solution, and it works like this:

- First, you're shown or convinced that you have a problem.

- Second, an emotional reaction, usually fear, is stirred up within you.

- Third, a grand solution is presented that will solve your problem and remove your fear when you sign on to their program or buy the product.

Nearly every television advertisement uses this approach. For example, an ad comes on showing a woman at a party in a black sweater. She looks down at her shoulders and sees tiny flakes there that have fallen out of her hair. In her distress, shame, and embarrassment, she urgently leaves the party. What is she going to do? How can she ever go back out in public with flakes? And in comes the shampoo solution. She uses it and smiles glowingly. In the next scene, she's at another party, and the other guests are giving her lots of attention, admiring her beautiful, shiny, healthy, flake-free hair. In the final scene, the man of her dreams is running his hands through her clean, sexy hair.

Problem-Reaction-Solution. Pay attention. You'll see it everywhere.

Internal problems cannot be solved through external solutions, but the ego thinks otherwise. Sophisticated marketers know this. That's why they tie their products, whatever they may be, to your emotional reactions and desire for security.

Our emotions are fueled by chemicals, drugs produced by our bodies. We can become addicted to these drugs. If we become conditioned to associate the warm fuzzy feelings inside us with a product or ideology, we'll buy more of the product, thinking that's what is making us feel good. It's pretty simple and pretty obvious when you become aware of it. It's an imaginary back-and-forth game between Heaven and hell, except thee are only superficial-ego problems with only superficial-ego solutions.

There are three major areas where we've really bought into this and where it can really mess up our ability to experience authentic love and inner peace.

## BIG MYTH #1:
## FINDING "THE ONE" WILL MAKE ME HAPPY

You may have found yourself thinking:

- He's "The One."

- I need to have this relationship.

- I need to get out of this relationship and find someone else.

- I am searching for "The One," and I'll know him when I see him.

- I should be married by now.

- I can't live without him.

If you've ever believed any one of these ideas, you've bought into one of the most emotionally destructive myths of all time. This myth is linked to the very popular notion of Soul mates. The concept of Soul mates generally infers that you are born onto earth with half a Soul and that someone else on earth has the other half. You aren't complete and can't be fully happy until you find your other half, and vice versa. Thus, your lifelong job is to search the earth, looking for your other half. Otherwise, you'll never be at peace and experience true love until you find this person. This is a classic ego notion that supports your stay in hell—it sets you up to seek and never find.

I believed in the one Soul mate idea in this form for many years. All that time, I felt an empty, lonely place in my heart that longed for the right woman to fill it up. It was rare, but about every 7-10 years, I'd meet a woman I thought was so incredible, so beautiful, and so much fun to be with that I knew she was the one for me. She was my type in every way, so I just knew I had finally found my Soul mate. I was on a huge high, in love, and convinced I was on the path to happiness ever after.

It was so wonderful for a time. Until something seemed to happen that would blow up all thought of ours being a perfect match. She'd find out something about me, or I'd find out something about her, or some behaviors would show up that neither of us could tolerate in each other, always something that showed our relationship wasn't the right fit. Whatever it was, the high would be gone fairly early on, and we would spend the rest of the time struggling to rekindle that wonderful, romantic feeling again— which wasn't coming back.

Falling in love is a lot like the first cup of morning coffee. When it initially hits your system, you feel so good, warm and energized and happy. Later, the euphoria fades. Then the rest of the day, you're drinking more and more cups, hoping to get back that feeling but it's gone.

After the first few times this happened, you'd think I would wake up from the experience and realize that this Soul mate thing wasn't working. Well, I didn't right away. In my despair, my friends, especially my female friends, would try to cheer me up by telling me things like "She just wasn't 'The One' or "Now you're that much closer to finding 'The Real One'. Don't give up. She's out there!"

Their experiences were just like mine, and they kept reinforcing the myth regardless of the apparent truth we all shared. Time and time again, I watched them proclaim they had found "The One," only to see the romance crash and burn a short time later. I know many people who have found "The One" at least three times; they've got the marriages and divorces to prove it. I myself have thought I found "The One" four times in my 43-plus years of life.

With all the experiential evidence contrary to this myth, why is it still being supported? Partly because it's juicy emotionally, it's big business, it's really big money, and the ego has no other way to even get close to Soul-connected love. This myth primarily appeals to and is sold to women. Men buy into it—I certainly did, but women are the main customers who are being sold on this.

Just the other day at the bookstore, I saw romance novels stacked several rows deep. When I asked a clerk if they sold very many, she said, "Romance novels make up more than 50% of fiction book sales, around $2 billion a year for the industry."

I continued to look around and counted 16 different bridal magazines on the rack. Guess how many magazines on the shelf were for the groom? Zero! I did a little more research and found that when the movie *Cinderella* came out, it was the largest grossing film in history at that time.

Then I checked my *Yellow Pages* and found over 500 listings under the bridal category. I discovered that DeBeer's sells over 6 billion dollars' worth of diamonds, even in a recession (*The New York Times*, February 2009), and the average American wedding ceremony cost around $28,000 (CNN-*Money*). However, the real shocker, for me at least when I added it up, was how much people spend every year on weddings—over $65 billion, and that's just in the US. So there are billions of reasons why this myth is so pervasive in our culture. It's exciting, seductive, and very profitable for some; but it is very destructive to your experience of Soul-connected loving if you're relating to it in the traditional way.

Believing and actively pursuing this myth actually keeps you from being happy. Here's why: It implies that you aren't worthy of love until you find "The One" who tells you that you are. This is very troublesome. It says, "You're not good enough" if you're not married. It tells you that you will always feel incomplete, afraid, and lonely until you meet your Soul mate. Or if your Soul mate ever leaves you, then you're destined to a life of incompleteness and depression.

Well, I felt incomplete, depressed, afraid, and lonely right up until the day I stopped believing in this myth.

Now, I'm here to joyfully tell you that this myth is just that— a myth, and there is another way to be filled with love. There is another way to experience the Soul mate concept. And the only reason I can say this is truth is because of the experience. The only real test we have to challenge a belief is our own experience, so use it and trust it.

If you have ever believed that someone was the reason for your happiness, you know the pain and deep feeling of disconnection that occurred when that person eventually fell short of your expectations. When you knew the relationship was over, it felt like someone had stolen your Soul, right? This pain can be unbearable. I know; I've been there. In some cases, it's the deepest of all psychic pain because it's the ultimate disconnection. This is no way to go through life and certainly not the way to love.

When we believe someone is our Source of happiness, what we've essentially done is make them God, the Source. This is the common idea of Soul mates. You're half and their half together makes you a complete spiritual being. And if you've made a person that powerful, you've disconnected from the Source that created you as you are. You've substituted a physical person for the Spiritual Source.

Even ancient scriptures warn against this. Two of the Ten

Commandments in the Old Testament state, "Thou shall have no other gods before Me" and "Thou shall not worship false idols" (Exodus 20:3-5). When you believe that someone has the sole power to rescue you, supply you with love, make you whole, and make your life worth living, you have made them your God. And if you believe they have qualities you need, you've made them your idol as well.

When you substitute a person as your Source for love and inner peace, you lose your connection with the Divine Source of love, and this is devastating to your psychological and spiritual well-being. This is what makes a breakup so painful.

Separation from the Divine Source puts you in hell, as we talked about in the previous chapter. Fear is the indicator of the separation. Metaphorically, if you've made someone your Soul mate (God) in your mind's eye and he or she happens to leave you, that means experientially you're going to be in fear, you're going back to hell.

This is why some people say, "I can't live without him." The physical world separation, the breakup, in your mind equates to a spiritual realm separation from Heaven because of the way you've got it wired in your psyche. This is why some breakups can be so terrifying and so painful. When a false god leaves, there is death, a death of an illusion that happens inside you.

It doesn't have to be this way. There is another way to understand and experience this. The affections of people can come and go, so you need to accept that. The part of yourself that feels incomplete when someone leaves is only made whole when you connect and align with the Spiritual Source. The hole that is left in your heart is in the shape of your Spiritual Power; that's "The One" we're all really looking for.

Once you understand and are able to connect to the Divine Source of love within yourself, you'll never feel beholden to another person for love again. Once you realize that the experience of love comes through you to the outside and doesn't come from the outside in, you'll really be able to share love in a much more fulfilling way and without all the painful drama.

Love, like a diamond, isn't a scarce commodity just because you believe it to be or just because others believe it to be. Did you know that miners dug 75,000 pounds of diamonds out of the ground in 2006 alone (*Smithsonian Magazine*, May 2008)? There is no shortage of diamonds or love. Once you realize this, you won't want to hold on to your love for the future for one special person; you'll want to give it away to others freely because you know the Source is unlimited.

Love doesn't work by the same principles of the physical world. In the physical realm, the more of your wealth you give away, the less you have. In the spiritual realm, the more you give away, the more you have. You'll see the Soul in your mate or partner as an inner essence of him, not all of him. You'll also see a flesh-and-blood human being with a mind of his own, struggling, fumbling, making mistakes, and doing what humans do. You'll be able to love him while knowing that he is not the Source of your love and inner peace. That Source is elsewhere.

And as you become more versed in Soul-connected loving, you'll love him knowing that the love you send out is its own reward, regardless of his ability to return it. You also start to see the Divine lovable essence in everyone. And when you see others as lovable beings, you will begin to have a full heart. You'll start to experience everyone as Soul mates, not as the Soul mate you need to complete you, but as mates that are spiritually connected by a thread of unconditional love. This doesn't mean you don't have a compatible partner that you love and are committed to. It just means you don't see this partner as the sole Source for your inner well-being.

Once you experientially understand that your worthiness isn't tied to the affections or presence of another person, that it's tied to a Spiritual Force, you become free. You realize you are worthy of love because you exist. Millions of complex biological and metaphysical events had to occur in miraculous harmony in order for you to be conceived, born, and grow to who you are now. The Universe put you here, and that is enough. That alone makes you worthy; you are part of the whole.

When you start to connect to the Divine Source of love, you'll know this is true. You'll experience it. It's just a matter of shifting your focus from the outer material world to the spiritual world within you.

## Big Myth #2:
## Success Will Make Me Happy and Bring Me Love

You may have found yourself thinking:

- I should be more successful than I am.

- I have to have that job.

- When I reach some more success, I'll then be able to have love.

- I am behind schedule on my life career plan.

- When my career takes off, everything will be good.

"You have to work hard to get somewhere in life" is what they say, but where is this "somewhere" we're supposed to be trying to get to? What is it we're really after with all our hard work?

Our society instills in us a belief that we are measured by our productivity. We are taught as children to compete at school for grades, in sports for the best playing position, and in the family for the affection of our parents. Much of the approval we receive as children is a result of our doing well at some task. We can't help but learn to associate doing well with love and affection—and associate doing poorly with being alienated or in trouble of some kind. "Santa Claus only brings gifts to good little boys and girls. The bad kids get switches and ashes" is what I heard as a child.

Eventually, we come to associate good and bad with winning and losing. The winners are good; the losers aren't good enough. The winners get the glory; the losers have to leave the celebration and go home humiliated. The deep underlying message we often get from this is: Only the winners are lovable; losers aren't lovable. Of course, people don't say that directly to us—"You lost the game" or "Your grades are low; you're not lovable!"—but this is often the message received psychologically. We reward winners with attention, affection, and prizes; the losers mostly get ignored, pitied, or punished.

As we become adults, we take this belief into our careers because we aren't taught how to accept our losses and still know we are lovable. If you spend much time watching television or movies, you can't help but witness and be affected by the glitz, glamour, and idolization of celebrities. Whether they're movie stars, pro athletes, or billionaires, they seem to have the love of the world, people seem to worship them.

On one level, we all want that kind of attention. We want to be loved and adored. Underneath all the tangible rewards of success, the one thing we really aspire to is gaining love and approval. Some of us are terrified that if we don't make it big, it will mean, "No love for you!"

In Western culture, you're taught to feel good about yourself if you work hard and to feel guilty when you don't. Early Judeo-Christian religious scriptures say, "For He gives to every man the reward of his work" (Job 34:11) and "Unto Thee, O Lord! belongeth

mercy: for Thou renderest to every man according to his work"
(Psalms 62:12). These quotes could be understood to mean the
harder you work at your job, the more God is going to love and
have mercy on you. This is how many of us have been conditioned.

Or they could be understood to mean the rewards come from
doing the Soul's work of spreading love and peace. Unfortunately,
it seems that the former idea has taken a deeper root in our society.
We've learned to tie our worthiness, happiness, and lovability to
our successes at our jobs.

Inside many of us is a tape that constantly runs, telling us that
happiness will come as soon as we get somewhere. This "somewhere" hangs in front of us like a carrot dangling in front of a horse
pulling a wagon. No matter how hard we pull, we can't seem to
reach the carrot. And if we finally do, we take a bite, find it unsatis-
fying, and move the carrot farther out, thinking we need to pull a
little harder this time to make it really satisfying. If you have set
a mark that must be achieved in order for you to feel good about
yourself, you can't help but wake up every morning in fear. Instead,
we need to wake up and see the irony of working so hard to make
life easy. The following story gives us insight into the concept.

## GETTING TO THE BEACH

—Author Unknown

*A retired, older businessman from Los Angeles was on
vacation in Mexico. While walking the beach, he met a local
man casually sitting in the sand, sculpting the most beautiful
piece of art the businessman had ever seen.*

*He approached the artist and said, "Your artwork is
amazing! I want to make you an incredible offer. If you
come back to LA with me, I'll help you, and you'll become
a success!"*

*The young artist said to the businessman, "What does that look like?"*

*The businessman excitedly replied, "If you come back with me and work really hard for 30 years, you'll be well known, respected, secure enough to retire, then you can come to the beach, have a home, do whatever you want, and enjoy the rest of your life like I'm able to do."*

*The artist smiled, quietly took another cut out of his wood, and said, "Thank you, that sounds wonderful. But I must tell you, my friend, my belly is full. I live right there next to the beach. All of these people you see in this town know me and are my trusted friends. I carve wood because I want to, and I enjoy my life every day. It seems I already have all those wonderful things you say I can have by putting in 30 years of hard work."*

If you look deep enough into human motivation, you'll find the desire to have love and peace as the ultimate driving force behind nearly everything we do. We want love more than riches; we just don't know this.

This force is so powerful that some of us will sacrifice just about everything—including our health, our integrity, our families, our relationships, our children, and what valuable time we have on earth—just to pursue professional goals, so we can prove our worthiness. We want to experience more love, and we unconsciously believe that more career success is the way to accomplish this.

There is nothing wrong with working hard and having career success. It's when we think it's going to get us some kind of inner approval that we're in psychological and spiritual trouble. I know men who've worked 14-hour days for 30 years to become rich, powerful, and hugely successful only to die of heart attacks a year or two after they retired. Some men believed that if they had success at work, made a lot of money, they'd get the girl; and if they got the girl, that would get them love. Well, they got the worldly success and the girl, sometimes several; but that feeling of love and inner peace they wanted wasn't there because that is not where love and inner peace are found.

I've known countless beautiful young women who set their sights on Hollywood movie stardom, not because they loved acting so much but because they wanted to be famous and be loved. I've known many men who've struggled for years to become successful, thinking that would get them the love and the appreciation they always wanted from their fathers. They spent so much time working, their fathers eventually died, and the relationships they wanted never happened.

The tragic drug overdose deaths of huge celebrities like Elvis Presley and Anna Nicole Smith can show us the shadowy side of fame and fortune. Their lives and deaths show us that no matter how much worldly success, fame, and money you have, without love of your Soulful self, nothing else matters.

Outer success doesn't equate to inner fulfillment. The infatuation and idolization from fans doesn't align you with the spiritual experience of love, and love is what we're really seeking. Many of us just don't know it.

## BIG MYTH #3:
## OWNING THE RIGHT STUFF WILL MAKE ME HAPPY

You may have found yourself thinking:

- I can't wait until I get that new _____.

- I should get a nicer car.

- I wish I had the things they have.

■ I have got to go shopping.

■ When I get _____, everything is going to be great.

At least once in our lives, we have all probably heard, "You can't buy happiness." So did we *really* hear it? Did it sink in? It doesn't appear so.

As I am writing this section, some of America's largest corporations are collapsing as a result of the actions of those that believed it could. Many of the top company executives are being indicted on criminal fraud charges for falsifying financial statements and insider trading.

Many of these people were already multi-millionaires, but apparently the money wasn't enough to get them where they thought they needed to be, to feel at peace. What did they need so badly that they were willing to sacrifice their lives, their reputations, and their freedom in order to get it? I believe it was love. They just didn't know that.

We are brought up hearing and reading messages that the things we can buy or own will bring gratification into our lives and take away the fears. The messages likely begin to work on our psyche when we are about two or three years old, when one of our baby friends grabs a toy away from us and screams, "Mine!" In that moment, we may have decided *that* toy was the one thing we really needed, and now someone else had it. "I've got to get it, or I'll be lacking!" is the trick our ego plays on us.

We see others with nice toys and think they're fulfilled, so we think we need toys like theirs to get some of that happiness for ourselves and that if we get a toy better than theirs, we will be even happier than they are. This is how our egos begin to blossom as we begin to equate ourselves with our stuff. The better the stuff, the better we are personally.

Later in life, it's not about toys anymore. It's about cars, dresses, shoes, diamonds, houses, neighborhoods, schools, and things like that. We learn to compare our things with the things of others, and we calculate our personal worth based on whose diamond is bigger, whose car is more expensive, and who designed the suits we're wearing. On one level, we're smart enough to know it's superficial and flawed; nevertheless, we get drawn into this way of thinking because it's all around us.

"Do you know what every woman needs to make it through the day? A good lipstick!" according to a national-run TV ad by a leading cosmetics company. Don't we wish that was all it took to make it through the day? A good lipstick? I think I would start wearing lipstick if that were true.

How about "Diamonds are forever"? I'm sure you've heard that one. A diamond. What a powerful enticement to secure the eternal love of your mate. If a man buys her a diamond, she will be his forever, and he will be hers forever. Or so the message infers. Owning the diamond is a symbol of owning the love of your mate.

The marketers can't give us what we really want, so they try to substitute their product instead. It's genius. What we really want is everlasting love. Because they can't sell us that, they sell us the symbol of everlasting love. Because we've been conditioned to equate the experience and feelings we want with a product, we go for the product. And we're willing to pay a lot of money for a little, bitty, clear rock because what it symbolizes is so important to us.

This one commercial is my favorite—"I love you, man!"— where two rugged men shed tears and a touching moment as one man hands another a beer and say he loves him. Beer equals love and good times with close friends. That is what the ad wants you to think anyway so that the next time you want to connect with your buddies, you'll think you need some beer to make that happen.

One morning while I was writing this book, I was interrupted by a very nice woman at my door who wanted to sell me vacuum cleaner. I told her I wasn't very interested, and then she asked, "Would having a clean house make you happy?"

I thought about that for a moment and then laughed out loud. She didn't have a clue what can of worms she was about to open, talking like that with me. I said, "Ma'am, I wish it would—."

She said before I could finish, "And each one comes with a three-year guarantee!"

I responded, "Guaranteed to make me happy for three years? Give me 20!" I figured I could live another 60 years.

For a second she lit up, thinking she might have a sale.

Then I lovingly looked her directly in the eyes and said, "If that vacuum was the key to our happiness, I would buy every one you have on the truck and give one to everybody I meet." She quickly realized that I was going to be a real pain and very likely not be a new customer.

Our conditioning can make us think that getting something new will elevate us to a higher level of enjoyment in our lives. Sometimes it does for a brief moment; but once the thrill of anticipation and newness (romantic period) wears off, we're back where we were. The moment doesn't last.

Products we seek cannot give us what we really want, even if they have a guarantee. A new car is nothing; it has no meaning to our Soul. A big house is nothing; it has no meaning to our Soul. Material things, even the shiny ones with designer labels, offer nothing of real inner value to our Souls.

There is often something behind the "item" that we are really seeking, and it's important that we stay aware of it. We have to realize that the thing we think we want may only be a poor substitute for what we really want.

Here is an exercise I often do with people who are unhappy and believe unconsciously that material gain is the path to their happiness. It's something that can help you discover what you're really after.

- So, what is it you want?

  *I want a new house to live in.*

- If you have a new house, what will that give you?

  *Well, I'll have a nice place to live, somewhere I'll be proud of showing to people.*

- If you have a nice place, what will that give you?

  *I want to have friends over. I want my family to be comfortable.*

- If you have friends over and a comfortable family, what will that give you?

  *It will be fun.*

- If you're having fun, what does that give you?

  *I don't know. Fun is sharing laughs, good times, just being together with each other. I enjoy being together with people.*

- So, what will that give you?

  *I'll enjoy my friends and my family more. I'll feel connected.*

I've done this exercise literally hundreds of times with people, and we always end up at the same place. If you take the question deep enough, the desire behind the material want is inevitably tied to the experience of some form of love, peace, and sharing. So the next time you think you really need some "thing," ask yourself, *What will this give me?*

Instead of being attached to making a house deal or new car deal or buying a new wardrobe or some thing you don't need, why don't you just go directly for what you want, cutting out the things that can't really deliver? When you ultimately want connection, go for connection above all else. The house deal can make or break, but you'll still have the option of enjoying friends and family no matter what else happens.

As it's been said, "A house doesn't make a home," only love and connection makes a home. Home is a place of connection and belonging, and that experience can happen anywhere.

## THE PROMISE OF HAPPINESS

Why is a new relationship, a new job, or a new wardrobe so exciting and intoxicating at times? It's easy to get very worked up about these things, especially a new romantic relationship, because in your mind these things promise you love and happiness. The operative word here is *promise.*

Your anticipation of a better future coming your way moves you to an emotional high. Many times, you can create a fantasy or a vision about what someone or something new is going to offer you. It's this anticipation, this promise of happiness that gets you excited. You may think that it's the person or thing that is the cause of your excitement, but it's really your own mind's fantasy that gets you so juiced. Your mind is expecting happiness to come, and you're excited about that—but there is a catch.

If you've ever fallen madly in love before or thought you had found someone who could make your life wonderful, you probably know what I'm talking about. Reality eventually showed up in a sobering way; the promise didn't deliver.

When you give your power away to a person, an event, or a

thing as a savior of sorts, you're in spiritual trouble. When you're thinking, *This person is going to make life wonderful* or *This job is going to give me everything I need* or *This house is going to change my life,* you're betting too much of your inner well-being on an outside circumstance. Outside circumstances are constantly changing; and if you rely on outside circumstances for your inner peace, your inner peace is going to be constantly changing as well.

The riches of the physical world can be great fun and make life comfortable for our bodies, but they won't give us that deep feeling of spiritual connection. Jesus talked about this two thousand years ago: "How hard it will be for those who have wealth to enter the kingdom of God! It is easier for a camel to go through the eye of a needle than for someone who is rich to enter the kingdom of God" (Matthew 19:24). Think of the kingdom of God as the place where love and peace reside inside you.

What Jesus is saying is that those who've focused their minds on the riches of the physical world miss what really matters to their hearts and souls. When you focus on riches, you will feel fear inside because your mind is moving away from the Source that really supplies you with peace.

It's not the riches that are the problem. It's your thinking that riches are going to make you happy that is the problem. It's the pursuit, desire, and belief that riches will offer you what you need. It's the mindset that is the problem.

This concept is something you can experience yourself. When you really want something or someone and think you have to have it, become aware of how much stress and anxiety this want is creating in your life. The more you have to have it, the more fear you feel and the farther away from peace you go. The more you want for the future, the less joy you have in the moment.

Think about your life. Romantic feelings have come and gone. Jobs have come and gone. All the stuff, the clothes, the toys, the cars, the parties, and the money have come to you at various times in your life. How much of it really delivered the way you hoped it would? From experience, we all know that those things can't fill the void inside us. Yet we still at times find ourselves believing and buying into it all and thinking, *This time will be different* or *This person is different* or *I just need a little more.*

It's time to stop coddling yourself with these myths and delusions. They won't work, no matter how many people tell you they will.

It's time to stop hoping that love will show up some day. It's time to start living with love right now.

Giving up hope doesn't mean you're giving up on love, just on the false delusions about love. The love and deep peace you want to experience is all around you. You just may be looking for it in all the wrong places.

## SEEKING THE SOURCE

If you stop thinking you need someone or something so your life can be better and if you start focusing on what you have right now, your anxiety will go away. The emptiness that feels like a hole in your heart is in the shape of your Higher Power, not Mr. Right and not a new toy or outfit. If you embrace and connect to your Spiritual Source for your fulfillment, you'll never feel alone and you won't feel afraid.

It doesn't necessarily mean you give away your home, your furnishings, your spouse, or your career—it means you take on a state of mind that is not attached to these for your sense of inner well-being. It means you can be fired from your job and not feel useless or inferior. It means your boyfriend or husband can leave you, and you don't feel abandoned or unworthy. It means someone can steal your car, and you don't feel lacking. Buddha taught, "One is the way to personal gain; the other, the way to Nirvana."

If you take the attitude *If it's meant to be, it will be. I've done all I want to do. It's in Spirit's hands now,* you will move closer to peace. If you start extending kindness, help, and love toward others around you right now, those feelings of fear and disconnection will go away.

When you find gratitude for what you have, those things you have will seem to expand. When you stop looking for love and peace in the future and start looking for it right here, right now, it miraculously shows up.

So when you start to think you really need someone or something, remind yourself that they're not your Source. Remind yourself that you are complete no matter what happens or doesn't happen. And that the way to the experience of love is by extending it from your inside outward.

## THE ULTIMATE SUCCESS

Ask a young man what success is, and his answer will likely be career-related. Ask a young woman what her ultimate success goal in life is, and her answer may likely be marriage- and children-related. Ask an enlightened, Soul-centered person what her ultimate goal in life is, and she'll likely say, "Love, connection, and inner peace."

What if you changed all your life goals to a focus on love, peace, and connection? What if you began to measure success by how peaceful and happy you were every day? What if you measured success by how wonderful you felt inside from helping and connecting with others? How would your life be different if you sought to accumulate memories of loving experiences instead of money and material trappings?

Success, the kind that is truly fulfilling, is measured by how much love, peace, and connection you experience inside yourself. No other measure even comes close.

There is a saying, "A rich man without peace has nothing he really wants; a poor man with peace has everything he wants."

Seriously consider this: If you have love and inner peace, you have no want for anything else. If you're at peace, then everything is fine just the way it is, right?

When you're at peace, you are in a state of mind that is free of want, free of judgment, and content with what is now. Peace comes from not wanting. And if you have peace, what else is there to have that will matter?

# Dismiss the Illusion That Romance Is Love

*True love is like ghosts,*
*which everybody talks about and few have seen.*

—Francois Duc de La Rochefoucauld

*W*e've been taught to believe that romance and the grand event of "falling in love" is the ultimate relationship experience. We've been taught to believe that love is something that just happens to us, that it is a magical experience that finds us. We expect to one day fall in love and have someone fall in love with us—we just don't know when or with whom, so we search for it in the eyes and faces of those we see, hoping to feel that magical feeling will come over us. "Does he have it? No? Well, how about him over there?"

We've learned that if someone shows up and we feel a certain wonderful, romantic way inside, this feeling is love and this relationship must have great significance because we feel this wonderful high inside. We believe that falling in love is some kind of supreme directive that requires us to change our lives, drop everything, and follow this feeling no matter what. We've been conditioned to think that it is such a precious event that we absolutely must pursue it at all cost.

Another common thing we hear is, "When the right one shows

up, you'll feel it and you will know." So, over time, we've begun to value romantic feelings as indicators of a relationship that is meant to be, God-created or Heaven-sent.

But does this romantic feeling really mean true love, or is it something else? If you want to move towards an enlightened, Soul-centered perspective, you need to fully understand the cause and effect of romance and the notion of romantic love.

## HISTORY OF ROMANTIC LOVE

If you were to look it up in the dictionary, you would find Webster's definition of *romance* to be: a long poem or tale originally written in one of the Romance dialects (Spanish, French, Italian, etc.) about knights; also a novel of love and adventure; excitement and love of the kind found in such literature. The word *romantic* is defined to be: of, like, or characterized by romance; fanciful or fictitious; not practical; visionary; full of thoughts and feelings of romance.

Our current understanding of romantic love has evolved out of ancient tales, poems and stories of knights, passion, and adventure. Its origins can be traced back a few thousand years in mythological stories. The ancient Greeks had Eros, the masculine god of love from which the word *erotic* stems. The Romans had Cupid; the Hindus have Kama; and in Buddhism, Mara is the demon that tempted Gautama Buddha with visions of seductive, beautiful women. These mythological characters all have very similar roles. They are all symbolically responsible for a passionate, desirous, physical, sexual kind of experience.

Mara is considered the spirit that leads one away from the path of enlightenment. Most of us are familiar with the image of Cupid, the round-faced, winged, baby boy who mischievously flies around shooting people with tiny arrows causing them to fall passionately in love with each other. Eros, Cupid, and Kama, although from different cultures of the world, are all winged boys who shoot passion-tipped arrows at unsuspecting mortals causing them to be struck dumb with passion.

In the myth, if you are one hit by the arrow, you receive a painful-yet-sweet wound. From this wounding comes an insatiable, fantastic, often crazed and lustful desire for someone. In this experience, there are feelings of blissfulness but also feelings of pain and fear because you can't quite get enough of what you want. You know what I'm talking about, right?

This insatiable craving, this need for someone is the root of romantic love's power. If you've ever been madly in love and thought you had to have someone, couldn't live without them, you know the power; it's an exciting experience. Yet there is often a sense of underlying fear and physical pain around your heart. It is from these early mythological stories that we have some of the first narrations leading into the development of the notion of romantic love.

However, romantic love as a reason to be together throughout most of the world's history is not commonplace like it is today in modern Western culture.

For thousands of years, marriages were arranged by families to serve social, political or practical reasons. Young men and women didn't date like they do now; they didn't carry on relationships with different partners waiting to magically fall in love with one of them. They got married when the family decided it was time. And forget about romance; these couples were forced together by family, societal tradition.

The church sanctified these unions, and the idea of marrying because you were in love wasn't a factor for consideration. The two people being married had little or nothing to say in the matter, especially the woman. Much of the world did, and some of it still does, consider women as personal property, and arranged marriages are still part of many traditions and religions.

During most of Western history, men have run the government and the churches and made the rules of law; so the idea of marrying for personal choice wasn't a luxury women had until fairly recently. This idea of romantic love, or marrying someone because you're romantically "in love" with them, is a relatively new proposition in its practice because for centuries women had no choice and no power. Passionate connections and sexual fulfillment was a luxury, and most women didn't have it.

And men didn't either in many cases; societal and religious tradition made the choice. Romantic love and physical attraction were absent in most married relationships. Sex was an obligation and the wife's duty to the man who supported her. So marriages were formed like business transactions. Couples were stuck, but women were especially stuck.

Under these frustrating, societal confines that endured for centuries, it shouldn't be a surprise that fictional tales of love, passion, and adventure became very popular. In came the romance story. People needed hope and a way to escape from a passionless existence. These stories gave them the relationship fantasy of what was missing in their everyday lives.

Joseph Campbell, author of *The Power of Myth*, credits the 11th-century French court poets/minstrels, the Troubadours, with popularizing romance and starting a movement towards romanticizing personal relationships. The Troubadours entertained the rich and while doing so created a game of romance with their songs and poetry.

It all would begin with a Troubadour writing poetry or singing a song inferring his desires and affections for the lady, often a married lady or a lady out of his social class. If she returned a subtle, interested response, the game of mystery, infatuation, lust, and intrigue would be off and running. The poet and the lady would then carry on a mostly one-sided romantic affair. It was an affair of words, but these were more than just ordinary words. These were artful, strategic craftings leading the lady to passion-filled fantasies.

In these affairs, romantic feelings ran high and were created with intent, not just by chance. The creative development of the fantasy—the suspense and the intrigue with the forbidden lover, was a skill the Troubadours sought to master. It was all in an effort to enhance the experience of what they called true love, or in French *fin amour*. It was a love that was found first with the eyes and then was felt with the heart. In these affairs, romantic situations and fantasies were designed, not natural.

The two would distance themselves so as to long for each other. From a window one might blow a kiss to the other, have a passing moment of lustful eye contact in a corridor, or have talk of a secret rendezvous in the garden at night. They would write dramatic letters and share in a fantasy of being together if only for an instant, knowing they could never realistically be together as a couple. It was love from afar, a forbidden, unavailable love, which made it that much sweeter and more tantalizing.

The Troubadours knew that people wanting something unavailable to them made them want it and fantasize about it that much more. It was this dance with wanting and longing for someone and not being able to fully have them that brought about much of the romantic feelings. This is also what brought on the pain. It was the separation from one another that allowed the imagination to run wild; and from this, anything seemed possible. And they knew this. The poets knew how to create the illusion of this experience and sought to hone their skills in making it more and more powerful. It was the Troubadour's belief that from this separation, the *fin amour* was able to flourish between the two souls.

These exchanges as a practice would prove to be historically significant. Probably for the first time in the Western world, women were glorified and idealized for themselves as individuals. They were respected, appreciated, and idolized for their beauty and feminine qualities. They were getting a kind of amorous attention and respect they had rarely experienced before this time. These women were enjoying mystery, excitement, adventure, and passion like women had rarely known or seen before with the men in their lives.

From this, an entirely new literary and story genre was being created. During this age, there was no television or cinema. Storytelling was the entertainment, and some of the most popular stories were those fictitious tales of knights, adventure, and love. There are many tales of knights slaying dragons or overcoming some ominous force in order to rescue a princess or young maiden. From these stories, the glamour of romantic love was being nurtured; and the Western world was embracing it enthusiastically. The Western world needed it because they were being strangled by their own boring, loveless, adventure-deprived traditions, and rigid social norms.

Over the centuries, these alluring tales and myths of romantic love have been re-created by some of the world's finest writers and storytellers. Shakespeare's famous *Romeo and Juliet* is a classic example of a romantic love affair. Romeo meets Juliet, and they fall instantly in love with one another; but they are forbidden to be together because of a longstanding feud between their families. Juliet fakes her death with a potion in order to escape an arranged marriage to another man she doesn't love. Unaware of her plan, Romeo comes upon Juliet, believes she is dead, and kills himself because he can't stand the pain of his thoughts of living without her. Juliet awakens from the potion, sees Romeo dead, then stabs and kills herself because she refuses to live without Romeo. Perhaps it is from this story that we've learned the myth that life is not worth living without "The One" true love of our life.

Probably the most recognizable and influential romance of our age is the story of *Cinderella*. It is widely known today as a Walt

Disney creation, but the story itself was written by Frenchman Charles Perrault in 1697. The Cinderella myth is one that has differing versions all over the world. It's basically the story of a young woman enslaved at home by her evil stepmother and evil stepsisters. She is rescued from that life of drudgery by the rich prince and goes on to be married in a lavish ceremony and live happily ever after.

In 1950, Walt Disney animated the story. At the time of its release, it was the largest grossing film of the year, around $4 million dollars. It's become one of the most popular fairy tales of all time. It's also gone on to become the blueprint of our dreams for our own real-life relationships, and marriages across the Western world emulate the prince and princess fairy tale-style wedding ceremonies with flowing white dresses, horse-drawn carriages, and extravagant celebrations.

This current popularized version of *Cinderella* is considered by many writers to contain the formula for the structure of a successful modern romance story. It is considered to have all the basic elements that would stimulate one's feelings of *fin amour* and make for a great romantic tale. These elements include an oppressed woman in need of help, a handsome—successful—desirable yet lonely single man who can rescue her from her fate, the promise of love and happiness if only they can be united, with a hopeful, happily-ever-after ending.

Many recently popular films use contemporary settings and characters but draw from these earlier-crafted romantic themes. Instead of princes riding up on white horses to rescue their maidens from imprisonment in tall towers like the story of *Rapunzel*, these modern stories have powerful business tycoons pulling up in limousines to whisk away their impoverished, unfulfilled, working girls to lives of passion, adventure, wealth, love, and fulfilling sex.

The modern story lines that you see everywhere in film and

romance novels have the same framework as these earlier romance tales. The same basic romantic strategies and techniques the Troubadours made popular a thousand years ago are still being used by writers as matter of regular literary practice today, and these stories are more popular than ever.

The history of the romance story has roots running deeply through our culture, so much so that many of us grew up with the understanding that experiencing romance was the only path to the experience of love; it was all we would see. What has happened over the centuries is we have taken a fictitious story like *Cinderella* and transposed it onto our own lives, making it our accepted understanding of how and where love is found. Somehow the understanding of desire, infatuation, and romantic fantasy has come to be our accepted notion of what love is.

Many of us want the romance, and we're looking for someone to rescue us from our own semi-loveless, unfulfilling, adventure-deprived lives. We want the Cinderella story to happen in our own lives, and we're not satisfied unless it does. We have been programmed by the entertainment industry and society to seek these fairy tale-style romantic relationships. We can't help it; it is what we've been shown, and it's what we are used to now. It's what we think will make our lives fabulous, just like Cinderella, rags to riches, in more ways than one.

But it doesn't really work that way, at least not for very many or for very long, because romance is an inherently fleeting experience.

Have you ever noticed that nearly all the romance stories and all the movies end with a "happily ever after" scene? The young couple's story ends when, after much struggle, they are finally able to happily be together. Just when their relationship is really beginning, the story is over. They go on to live happily ever after, out of our sight.

What about the rest of their lives? We don't get to see that part of the story. It's always left to our imagination.

And this is where the problem lies in our real-life relationships. We've been taught how we're supposed to "fall in love" and get married, but we're not taught anything about how to really love or sustain love from that point onward. We are left to our fantasies, and fantasy is not the real love experience.

## THE TRICK ROMANCE PLAYS

We're conditioned to believe that romance is something that is magical, supernatural, and divinely meaningful when you experience it with someone. But the truth is, romance can be created. Romance in our culture is experienced as a mix of excitement, passion, fear, adventure, and imagination.

When our normal, often ordinary, everyday lives are suddenly jolted awake by someone who takes us to the edge of our comfort zone, or who appears to have all the things that we think will give us the life we want, or who takes us to places we've never been before. This often creates feelings of romance inside of us. Romantic love is about having exciting, stimulating, new experiences with someone while believing he is the source or cause of that inner experience.

Successful romance novelists, romantic comedy writers, playwrights, and film producers have learned how to master the techniques to create romance just as the Troubadours did a thousand years ago. If you've ever been moved to tears by a touching story or a dramatic love scene on a screen, you've been manipulated towards this feeling by skilled writers, actors, and directors. The way they created, told, and formed the story moved you emotionally. It's not magic, but it feels like it sometimes.

If an artificial media like a book, film, or song can move us to a romantic experience inside our thoughts, then we know that romance isn't only caused by the presence of some special "perfect fit" person in our life, even though we tend to project that when we fall romantically in love with someone. We tend to think that it's the other person that causes this feeling, but it's really within our own minds and bodies.

The experience of romantic love is an illusion of the ego. Because the mission of the ego is to keep us from experiencing real love, connection, and peace, what better way to do it than by giving us a substitute for the real thing? The ego is always looking for a way to satisfy its needy self, as long as it doesn't have to really love anyone. If it looks, feels, smells, and taste like love, which romantic love can initially, we think it must be the real thing; but it is because of all these similarities that the world has fallen victim to a masterful deception.

It is a lot like a magic trick. A well-presented magic trick has charm, mystery, and a brilliant element of romance. If done properly, you can't see anything that might cause you to believe it's a trick. It appears that something supernatural is occurring.

Once you see the mirrors or catch some sloppy sleight of hand, it's all over. It loses its magical charm, and the romance of the trick falls flat, a lot like many of our romantic relationships.

## BEING IN LOVE VS. BEING TRULY LOVING

What is the difference between being in love and being truly loving? Being "in love" with someone is wanting him; being "truly loving" is wanting the best for him.

Think about that for a while. There is a dramatic difference in intention. Spiritual teacher Marianne Williamson puts this question to people struggling with their romantic relationships: "Do you want him to be at peace, or do you want him to call?"

When you are "in love," you want him to call, need him to call, sometimes desperately. If you want him in order to feed your own craving, you are in a fearful place; you're seeking his love to fill an empty place inside you.

On the other hand, if you truly want him to be happy and at peace and you aren't worried about him not calling or giving you attention, then you are in a "truly loving" place.

This is a critical difference, and it will make or break a relationship in time.

When you find yourself "in love," the emotional feelings associated with the initial stages of the relationship can be rewardingly overwhelming. It can be a state of exuberance, joy, and blissful excitement with anticipation of what's to come. It's a sense of elated confidence and well-being. Your body feels alive and healthy. Your mind is carefree and bright. You believe your partner is wonderful and see yourself as wonderful, even though you may not be consciously aware of that.

This experience mimics Soul-connected love, or real love, in nearly every way on an emotional and physical level. In this state you are not only in love with another, you are in love with yourself. This is the magic—a sense of oneness, optimism, and aliveness within you. It feels so much like the real thing that you are convinced it is real love. However, subtle differences often go overlooked. There are a few big clues.

### ✦ Fantasy

This is the core of romantic love. If you've ever fallen "in love at first sight" or thought you found "The One" after a brief meeting, you may know this already. When you see someone who is gorgeous and appears to be the personification of all your dreams rolled up into one person, wow! You're hooked. You feel desire, lust, excitement; your heart beats faster. You feel fear, nervousness; your palms sweat, and your mind races. You think, *This is my perfect dream match!*

Then you meet, and he is very charming, seems to have everything. You plan a date, and you await his call. Now is when the real romance begins. In your head. Your mind creates pictures and plays out fantastic romantic scenes with this person you hardly know. You start to picture all your wants, perhaps traveling together, having a home and children together, wonderful sex, and the sharing of an adventurous, joyous life together.

The more your imagination runs wild, the more you feel you have to have this man, the more you believe that he holds some kind of special power or, as some say, "the key to my heart." Because this person looks and seems like he might be a perfect fit for your dream romance, you insert him into that role. This person may not ultimately fit that role, but you put them there anyway because you're intoxicated by romance. You want it so badly and it feels so good, you tend to overlook the finer points.

As long as you keep a distance, maintain some mystery, hold some suspense, and long to be reunited, the romantic fantasy remains high. This is why many long-distance relationships can seem so perfect in the beginning and often fail immediately once the couple lives in the same town together. In many cases, the less time spent with someone, the more romantic tension builds and the deeper you fall in love.

It is the parts unknown and mystery that adds the flavor and excitement. It is in this empty space that your imagination creates and sets the scene for what's hopefully to come with this person, and I put great emphasis on "hopefully."

Romance is often our projection of our own personal fairy tale onto our current relationship experience. We're not in love with a real person; we're in love with what we want him to be or what we believe he is based on our fantasy. We're mostly in love with what could be. We're in love with the fantasy itself.

Soul-connected love, real love, doesn't need fantasy in order to accept another or find acceptance for one's self. When you experience real love, you can love someone in the present moment with whatever is happening right now. This experience of love isn't based on what a relationship could be or what this other person may be; it's based on what is, in this very moment. It sees the person, sees the situation, and feels an unattached fondness for what is.

### ✦ Urgency

Romantic love is urgent. Romantic love is a highly emotional, often highly sexualized, and often desperate desire to be with one's lover. Like in Shakespeare's story of Romeo and Juliet. Their passion for one another was so urgently overwhelming and the idea of not being together was so feared, Romeo took his own life rather than live without Juliet. If only he had relaxed a moment and caught his breath, things would have turned out differently.

When you feel you have to see him, have to get him on the phone, and waiting with the unknown is painful, this is not love—this is need; this is a wounded ego trying to be filled by the presence of someone. The ego also projects or sees qualities in others while telling you that you need some of that to be happy now.

Your ego, like a parasite, survives on the beauty, success, charm, life, and attention from another. Your ego will tell you that you don't have certain qualities on your own and must get them from someone else or at least be close to that. Or it may tell you that you have to get someone's approval before you can be lovable. And the ego can't wait to have all this, which is why some rush to get married. They want to hold on to, control, and capture this love so it doesn't get away. This urgency reveals the insecurity that underlies romantic love.

Soul-connected love doesn't get away or leave you when someone leaves because you have it inside of yourself. It has no need to hurry things up because it's not insecure.

Love is an abundant commodity; the more you give, the more you have to give. When you love someone, you can love him no matter where he is or whom he is with. Real love has no need to hurry anything because it accepts what is now and what will come. Real love is without fear. Real love doesn't feel jeopardized if someone is unavailable or if a phone call isn't returned right away. Real love is peaceful, solid, and secure.

## ✦ Temporary

The most romantic aspect of most relationships is the beginning, usually the first 12 months, or in the time before we really get to know the other person well, or before the relationship becomes habitual. Sometimes the romance will last a few years on its own, but rarely much longer without effort. During this initial time in a relationship, it's common to work a little harder on impressing our partner. We try to put our best side forward and tend to hide the things we don't want others to see right away.

Romance, although fun and very juicy for us emotionally, doesn't last on its own. It can't because eventually the ego mind will push through and turn against the person it so desperately needed in the past. When it no longer sees the potential or begins to see human imperfections, it starts to pick the other person apart and the romance is gone, along with thoughts and feelings you thought meant you were in love. When you hear someone say, "I am so in love with So-and-so," you can usually count the days before the heartache and disappointment arrive. Some will say it's cynical to expect romantic love to fail, but it's the nature of romantic love to fail.

Real love causes you not to care about how long those romantic feelings last or what kind of form your relationship takes. Real love endures and celebrates whatever comes. Authentic love lasts and is there by intention; it doesn't disappear when the physical, chemical, and emotional enticements change. Love sees the beauty in one's Soul and one's being regardless of external changes. Real love is an enduring experience even though the relationship may take on a different form or purpose. Real love lasts by your own intention to maintain that experience.

The relationship in its romantic form may dissolve, it may develop cracks, someone may leave; but the real love experience can still exist through all of that.

### ✦ Conditional

If you or anybody you know has ever been "in love" one day and some time later says, "I'm just not 'in love' with him anymore," then you know the limits of romantic love. With romantic love, the situation has to play out according to your desire and fantasy. When it doesn't, which is inevitable in time, you fall out of love. With romantic love, eventually the young prince riding the white stallion will be seen as an average Joe walking a mule.

The infatuation that we often confuse as love seems to be there as long as everything goes right according to your way of thinking; but when it doesn't, the infatuation stops. When the person you are in love with does things you consider intolerable or wrong, the romantic love you once felt fades away. I have often heard people say, "After we got married, he changed."

Most of the time he hasn't changed; he has likely always been who he is now. It's the fantasy of how you saw him that has changed. The magic spell of the fantasy wore off, and the real person was able to be seen for the first time. And when the real person, not the Prince Charming, is standing there, romantic love has a hard time enduring this newfound reality.

Real love accepts people as they are. It has no need or want to change anyone in order for love to be experienced. When you experience real love for someone, it is not conditional on how they behave at the moment or treat you or whether or not they give you what you want all the time. Real love causes you to seek and choose to see the real beauty in someone, not the flaws. Real love is experienced from a place of inner security and stability without the need of another offering something in return.

### ✦ Exclusive

When you're romantically "in love" with someone, it's not okay for your partner to love anyone else. Romantic love is jealous because it believes that love is scarce and must be protected. Because fear is at the root of this false love, you want to guard what you think you need, which is this other person.

Just like a hungry stray dog protecting its food source, you think that if your partner loves someone else that you'll go hungry. When in this state of consciousness, you don't believe you can replace this love. You're desperate to hang on to it and terrified of it slipping away. But this never works in relationships. Dependency on another is not loving, it's needing; and the Soul doesn't flourish behind locked gates.

Soul-connected love is not scarce and expands when experienced. This love thrives when it includes others and allows for freedom. Love is present when fear is absent. When in a truly loving state, you are not threatened by others; you realize that there is enough love for everyone. You know the importance of your partner sharing love with others for the benefit of his own soul and for the benefit of the entire community. I'm not talking about sex. Don't get the two confused. I'm talking about unconditional love. Soul-connected love is inclusive of everyone and to be shared.

### ✦ Ambitious

Romantic love wants to know, "Is this relationship going anywhere?" We've been conditioned to believe that romantic relationships should progress a certain way. You meet someone, you date, you fall in love, you get engaged, you get married, you buy a home, you have kids, you buy a bigger home, you remodel the kitchen, and so on. The ego has to keep acquiring and achieving its goals in order to believe it's worthy; love in the moment isn't enough.

When you think a relationship has to be moving towards a specific goal or achieving certain marks, it's often because you experience a lack of love in your current inner experience. By moving forward, your ego believes you will be brought closer to feeling peace, security, and more love; but it will never happen that way, no matter where your relationship goes. The ego will tell you that experiencing inner peace is not enough. It will tell you to avoid peace in the moment and keep things moving towards something perceived as better or more.

However, when you truly love someone and experience love together, nothing else seems important. An outer accomplishment doesn't equate to inner fulfillment, and the Soul knows this. Real love causes you to be at peace with yourself, with what you have now, and with where you are now. It has no outer goals, no ambitions. When in the experience of a loving connection, you have no other agenda but to experience the moment.

## ✦ Me-Centered

Romantic love wants to know, "What am I going to get out of this, or what am I going to get in return?" When we are in this false love state, we want something from our partner; we are in a state of lack and need. Romantic love is fueled by need and the belief that someone else can fulfill that need. You see him as having something you want; and as long as he can provide that, you think you'll be content. If he can't, resentment begins to swell.

When in this state of being, you don't think about the well-being and needs of your partner; you put yourself and your own needs first. You see your partner as someone whose job is to pacify your fears and insecurities. You see your partner as someone who is supposed to rescue you or save you, just like the prince in the fairy tales. Romantic love is parasitic, it wants to use someone, exhaust their resources, and when those are depleted, move on to find another host.

Soul-connected love looks at situations as "How do we all benefit from this?" When in a state of Soul-connected love, you look for win-win solutions and consider others as yourself. When in a state connected to real love, you aren't in need; you are in a state of inner abundance and want to give. You don't need to be saved because you've saved yourself through your connection to a divine source of love inside you. And from this state, you are able to share that loving abundance with others.

## WHY ROMANCE FEELS LIKE LOVE

In the realm of romantic love, physical attraction and physical contact can create sensations within us that we equate with love and strong feelings of intimacy. The simple act of directly looking into the eyes of someone you find attractive for a period of time longer than what is generally comfortable causes the body to release various chemicals into the bloodstream that can change the way you feel while creating a greater attraction. Try it sometime, and you will feel something happening inside you.

One of the many chemicals released during the initial attraction phase is named phenylethlamine, or PEA. PEA is related to amphetamines, which are stimulants that create the feelings of energy, strength, and well-being. This chemical, known as the "love drug," will give you a high. The right dose will make your heart rate increase, make your palms sweat, and can give you the feeling of butterflies in your stomach. It is a mood elevator and has been found to help reduce symptoms of depression.

This drug, as well as others the body releases, gives you a wonderful feeling that puts you in a stimulated, aware, sometimes blissful state. If your body can almost instantly be affected by powerful drugs like PEA just from gazing into someone's eyes, imagine what kind of chemical dosing you get from the intense physical contact of fulfilling sex.

One of these drugs that seems to have great significance within this realm is oxytocin. This chemical found in mammals is released during orgasm in both men and women. Yet it is generally much higher in women, especially during vaginal and nipple stimulation from sex or when giving birth or breastfeeding children. It is believed to be the chemical that facilitates the physical-level bonding experience between a man and woman and between mother and child. The release can subsequently be stimulated through the physical senses.

We, our bodies, can literally become chemically addicted to another person. We become like Pavlov's dogs that began to salivate when the scientist rang the bell before he fed them. Our bodies become conditioned and respond unconsciously to certain stimulation. Instead of our mouths salivating in expectation of food, our hearts beat faster, and we feel euphoric.

This would explain why it can often be so difficult for some people to break up with their partners, even when they know the relationship is really harmful for them. This can be a very dangerous addiction for you if you're trying to escape an abusive partner but you're chemically stimulated by his presence. You may feel no real mental or spiritual connection, yet you can be physically overwhelmed by the drugs your own body produces.

If you are in a relationship situation and you want out but feel strangely hooked on this person, you must get away from this person physically and stay away. Voice, smell, taste, and touch will trigger you physically to want to return. If you want to break the spell of your biochemistry, don't have contact where your senses will be stimulated. In situations like this, it may be best to have no contact with that person until the chemical release shuts down.

And in time it will. The high that any drug produces is temporary, another reason why the romantic love experience is a transient experience.

This internal chemical bath that affects us physically and emotionally often causes us to think that it is love we're feeling. However, many times it's not really love; it's just physical infatuation combined with a very complex biological urge to reproduce, attach, and protect offspring.

Because we're being literally swept up in our own drug-induced high, we want to think that it's a truly loving experience, but it may not be. For many years, I used illicit drugs and alcohol to get a similar feeling. The drug high emulates the feeling that love gives us but without the lasting sense of peace and well-being. The drug-induced bliss has many side effects that can really mess up our lives. Soul-connected love does not have negative side effects, but being in an addicted, dysfunctional relationship does.

Sometimes, it's hard to tell if you really love someone or if you're just powerfully attracted to him. If you aren't sure, honestly ask yourself:

- If this person wanted to stop seeing me or stop having sex with me, would I feel desperate in any way?

- Do I feel addicted to this person and not able to keep my boundaries or commitments to myself?

- Are my thoughts in conflict with my emotions and physical desires (Is my mind telling me one thing and my body another?)

- Is this relationship generating negative consequences in my life?

If you've answered *Yes* to any of these, you may be under a chemical spell of your own body's making. You may think you love this person but may in truth be attached to him because of the chemical or emotional high you get.

And this high doesn't always mean it's a pleasurable high. Sometimes, you can be addicted to someone who triggers your pain, but this drama and pain distracts you from a more painful emptiness deeper inside. The physical attachment combined with your programmed belief system around romantic notions of love often make it very difficult to distinguish between what is a purely physical-level experience and what is a truly loving, spiritual, Soul-level experience.

## Ego-Centered Sex vs. Soul-Centered Sex

Our human desire for sex is a very powerful one. It's programmed into us and, like the desire for food, it's a must for our survival as a species. Also like our hunger for food, it cannot be repressed for long. The more it is repressed, the more it wants to come out side-ways, in some kind of secret or shadowy way.

There are a lot of rules that we've been taught about sex. A lot of them are conflicting, without merit; some are entirely false. Sex has been demonized by religions and cast as shameful at times by society. Because of this, it's common for us to have wounds and lots of confusion around sex.

It's common to carry guilt and shame around sex, but you don't have to carry that. You can let that all go and come to a different understanding about sex and how it works and doesn't work in your own life. You can know this through your experience.

To keep this very simple, there is sex with love and sex without. Sex with love means you genuinely care for your partner and his or her best interest. Sex is a sharing of love and affection, and it's an experience that fills your heart. Inside yourself, you know you are okay and that you are taking care of yourself and another.

On the other hand, sex that is used to fulfill or satisfy yourself without conscious regard for your own well-being or the well-being of another is ego-centered. Sex from this place is about getting something for you; it's about making yourself feel better, whether it be better emotionally or physically, without regard for consequences.

Ego-centered sex is often about satisfying an inner need to be worthy. It comes from a place of "my needs first." If you've ever had sex and felt an emptiness or faint fear deep inside, this is a clear sign love wasn't present. Ego-centered sex wants to get the high, experience a temporary escape, and feel the physical closeness of another person without getting too close to be truly intimate.

And by intimate, I don't mean naked, although there is a level of vulnerability and openness that comes with that. What I mean by truly intimate is true sharing, realness, and revealing of who you are inside while accepting who your partner is. Intimacy is an openness and realness about who you are. I once heard intimacy rephrased as "intomeyousee." It's about being completely truthful about who you are, what you feel, and what you think in the moment. It's about being real.

Ego-driven sex can be physically intimate without being emotionally, mentally, or spiritually intimate. When you are not balanced within all the levels, this is when you feel guilt, fear, and regret. Even though you may be physically close with someone during sex, you feel separated from them and your own Soul. This is when sex can be harmful to your psyche.

Ego-centered sex is what those who are "sex addicts" engage in regularly. Because they don't feel a genuine love for themselves, they feel disconnected from the Spiritual Source; they seek relief and self affirmation through sex. They don't get the affirmation and connection they seek, but they do get a temporary escape with sex that momentarily pacifies the inner angst they feel. The high soon wears off; then back comes inner angst and the search for more sex.

The pattern repeats itself over and over again until they make peace with whatever wound it is they carry inside.

If you are seeking the experience of love and peace from sex, you've got it backwards. Sex is most rewarding when love is already present within you and sex is an expression of that love. Soul-connected sex is conscious; you consider another and yourself equally. When in this place, you do not seek to get something; you seek to give and share. Soul-connected sex isn't used as a tool to get something you want, whether it is a feeling or something material. You don't see another as an object that can offer you some thing you need; you see another respectfully as a soulful being first and physical-sexual being second.

Soul-connected loving doesn't mean you can't experience romance and sexual passion in the relationship. It means you don't seek romance and passion as a means to give you love.

Physical closeness doesn't bring you to the experience of spiritual connection. Soul-connectedness allows you to enjoy romance and the physical aspects of sex fully while knowing that sex by itself is not the path to inner fulfillment. Soul-connected sex is simply sex with a loving, non-judging, open, and giving heart.

# CHAPTER 5

# Choose Your Relationship Experiences

*No one can make you feel inferior*
*without your consent.*

—Eleanor Roosevelt

$\mathcal{I}$f someone says something mean to you and your feelings are hurt, who is responsible for your hurt feelings? If someone rudely cuts you off in traffic, scares you, nearly causes you to crash your car, and you get angry, who is to blame for your anger? The common response to these questions is, "They are. It's their fault I feel this way. They made me feel like this!"

But is this really true? Can someone else really be responsible for your feelings? This mindset of "I'm upset because of you!" is at the core of many relationship problems. It's the conditioned understanding that if you are upset, someone else has made you that way, someone else has put you in that bad mood.

Have you ever heard people say things like this? "I'm so angry because of what he said to me!" or "What he did really hurt me!" or "She really makes me mad!" Statements like these are things I hear every day. I have also witnessed highly trained professional psychologists ask their patients, "How does he make you feel when he does that?" The operative part of statement is the "he make you feel" part.

Just this morning, I heard a woman on the radio telling of her frustration and how, over the phone, a guy at the cable company made her cry. It has become so accepted to blame others for one's own inner upset that it has become an automated response that nearly everyone buys into. We are trained and conditioned daily to believe this.

## IDENTIFYING THE POWER WITHIN

There is a saying you may have heard as a child: "Sticks and stones will break my bones, but words will never hurt me." This school-yard saying holds a lot of truth. The lesson is obvious—someone can hurt your physical body with violence, but they can't harm your psyche with their words. As children, a good many of us heard this saying but chose not to learn the lesson when we were teased by other kids; we chose to be offended or hurt instead. We chose to listen to their ugly words or interpret their actions in such a way that we felt rejected, disrespected, and uncared for.

As an adult, you may still choose to be offended or hurt by certain remarks and actions of others. You let others affect your self-esteem and self-worth. You listen to their words and believe their opinions of you have merit. But you don't have to let them be the judges of how worthy you are. You don't have to let them affect how you are going to feel.

Thinking that others have the power to make or break your mood completely gives away your inner power. You become a puppet if the whims, judgments and biases of others determine your well-being. It makes you a victim. The big problem with being a victim is you don't take charge of and responsibility for your own life choices. By not taking responsibility for your own choices, you stay small, you live small, and you never feel connected because you see yourself at the mercy of others. When you allow others to dictate to you how you are going to feel, you are living as a slave with whoever is directing your mood as your master. Who do you want to be your master?

If you've ever been on the other side of this, someone else blaming you for his emotional upset, you know it can be a very uncomfortable place to be. When someone says you hurt him and made him feel bad, what can you do?

You can't fix his emotions. Sometimes there is absolutely nothing you can do. Sometimes your behavior or choices that you must make in order to live your life with Soulful integrity are not going to agree with someone else's. And because of this, he may feel hurt, offended, or rejected; but this is really his issue to work through, not yours. You are not responsible for his reaction any more than he is responsible for yours.

There was a time in my early twenties when I had just recently begun dating a woman. In the beginning, I was completely enamored with her as she was with me, but her interest soon changed, probably because I became desperately interested and too emotionally affected by her. We dated a few months, and then she started seeing someone else. She lied to me about it because she was probably afraid of hurting me or of my reaction.

When I found out anyway, I *was* very hurt and angry. And I blamed her for everything I felt. I blamed her for ruining my trust in women. At the time, I thought she wrecked my life and that I wouldn't ever be happy again.

All I could think of was how wrong and evil she was for doing this to me: *How could she take my heart, lie to me, betray me, and cause me so much pain!* I felt hate for her inside me and believed that she owed me. I thought she had to do something to correct this and that only she could fix my pain. I thought she would have to apologize, come back to me, and try to make things right.

Well, she never did anything to fix my pain, but she did go on to live her life. She was just living her life and not giving me what I thought I needed from her. She was living the path that was meant for her and making choices as best she could.

But I didn't like it. I thought she owed me respect, love, caring. I had to realize that she didn't owe me. I had to learn that my emotional reaction and upset was all mine.

She didn't hurt me. I hurt myself by not loving myself enough or loving her enough to let her be who she is.

Just because she lied to me doesn't mean I'm any less. Just because she chose another man doesn't mean I can't be happy for her and myself. Her not being the way I think someone should be doesn't mean I have to be hurt and upset about it.

When I finally decided to stop blaming her and stop beating myself up, I found a love for her, and I felt at peace once again.

Nobody wants to be responsible for your emotional well-being any more than you want to be responsible for someone else's. It's a scary burden for someone to be given the power over you emotionally. Few things will make a healthy person run away from you faster than your allowing them to make or break you emotionally.

You may think you aren't pointing the finger at others for how you feel, so I challenge you to take a look at how you are affected by their words and actions. The next time you have any strong emotional reaction, become angry, frustrated, disappointed, sad, hurt, ask yourself, *Am I making someone else responsible for my reaction or upset?* If you are, now is the time to reclaim your power. Here are two great ways to do that.

## 1. Choose to Not Be Offended

Even though you may not be used to making it a choice, you can choose to not be offended by others. You can choose to not be a victim.

You don't have to interpret someone's actions and comments in a way that is hurtful to you. You can choose to see and experience it another way. Being hurt or offended is a choice. Being at peace and unaffected is a choice. You may think you're not in charge of your emotions and reactions, but you are; you just have to learn how to relate to yourself in a different way.

For example, let's say we're friends, but I call you a lying, cheating, no-good car thief, and say that I want to have nothing to do with you. You'd probably have little reaction, right? This comment would likely not upset you one bit. But why not? I'm being critical, aggressive, and I'm rejecting you; that should hurt.

The reason you wouldn't take offense is because you solidly know you are not a lying, cheating, no-good car thief. It's a totally false and ridiculous statement. It doesn't trigger any particle of truth or belief inside you, so you decide it doesn't apply to you and you choose not to react.

But what if I said something else, something that hit you closer to home, something that you have a wound around, some area where you are not so confident within yourself? This insecure spot is commonly called your "button," and when someone pushes your button, it hurts. You get upset, and you think it's his fault because he pushed it. But it's not; it's your button.

This button was likely installed years ago as a childhood wound or trauma, but it's still sticking out there to be pushed by your old and new relationships. What can someone say or do that really pushes your button?

For the sake of discussion, let's assume you have a sensitive button about being overweight or fat. This is a common one that many people are very sensitive about. Many of us carry wounds around our personal appearance. So when someone says, "You look like you've gained some weight," you'll feel hurt and humiliated; your button gets pushed. You choose to take offense and think it was very rude that this person said that ugly thing to you and hurt you.

But let's assume it's true you have gained a few pounds. They are simply making a neutral and true observation, but you put your own hurtful, negative spin on it. You don't like that you've gained weight; you are not happy with yourself in this area, so you get upset and blame the other person for the thoughts and feelings you are already carrying about yourself.

Another person who hears those same words might say, "Thanks for noticing. I've been trying to gain a few pounds." So it's not the words that someone else says that stings so much. It's the beliefs you carry about yourself that their words remind you of that stir you up.

It's not their fault or responsibility that you carry around these beliefs about yourself. It's when their words trigger something that you deny or haven't accepted about yourself that you feel the inner sting. The difference between totally disregarding a statement as false and feeling hurt by a statement is how you think and already feel about yourself.

It's not what someone else says or does that really matters. It's *what you think about yourself* that gives their words or actions power. So let yourself off the hook, stop beating yourself up, and turning the words of others against yourself. When you start thinking better of yourself, what others say or do will have little effect on you. They will have little power over you.

Only you can uninstall your button.

## 2. Choose to Stop Defending Yourself

When we believe that someone is being inconsiderate, intrusive, or rude, the typical reaction for many of us is to take it personally and defend ourselves. A defensive mindset escalates fear and the body's production of adrenaline, further increasing your uneasiness.

This response usually isn't necessary and often escalates the separation from another that you already feel. The way to reconnect is to not defend and protect yourself. It's radically counter to what the outside world subscribes to, but it works for staying at peace within.

When you are solid in yourself, safe in your connection with your Soul, you have no need to defend your honor, opinions, or good name. You are calm inside. You are above proving you are right or good enough because in the eyes of your Soulful self, you already are good enough.

When you are secure in this place, you don't have to defend anything. When someone says something critical to you, you could respond by thinking, "Isn't that interesting that you would say that," and not take it personally and not get drawn into the conflict. When you decide you are not going to be offended by others, you can also decide it is not necessary to defend yourself.

Jesus said, "But I tell you who hear me: Love your enemies. Do good to those who hate you. Bless those who curse you. Pray for those who mistreat you. If someone strikes you on one cheek, turn to him the other also" (Luke 6:27-29). With these words, Jesus taught that true power comes from within. And when you are connected to that Source of inner loving strength, you have all that you need. No person can take that away or give that to you; so there is no reason to protect your opinions, good name, or honor. You don't need the good opinion of others to determine your self-worth.

By blessing others and not retaliating, you are able to take yourself to an even higher level of loving consciousness; you are able to control your own level of peace. What others think about you is really none of your business.

However, the ego believes you have to be right, uphold your opinion, and prove yourself in order to be okay. The thought of being wrong threatens the ego's worthiness. This is why some people argue and fight so aggressively, like their lives depend on it. For those who live in their insecure egos, their ego's life does depend on it. But you don't have to defend yourself just because you are up against another's desperate ego. When you know you are right within yourself, you really gain nothing by trying to prove it to others. If anything, it draws you into a lower level of energy.

And in not defending yourself at every turn, your self-esteem will improve and your relationships will change because your mind will be focused on loving thoughts and not fearful thoughts. If you want more peace in your life, you have to demonstrate more peace. You have to practice letting the petty gossip and inconsequential attacks on you go by without being affected or drawn into the cheap conflict. The ego is constantly on the attack. It's up to you whether or not you get drawn into the conflict.

If you are constantly being triggered by the behavior and words of others, the work is not to change them but to change yourself. If you look inside yourself instead of protecting yourself, you will find that place you have yet to make peace with. Perhaps it's a very old wound from the past or a fear that you have let go unfaced. If you really want to be at peace with the world, you have to first be at peace with yourself and love this wounded area inside you.

The enlightened perspective is one of personal responsibility. At times, you are going to feel hurt and upset. This is fine and okay; experience it fully. But don't blame others for it. These feelings are yours inside of you; nobody gave them to you. You have the power to release these painful emotions and embrace something new.

You can choose to think and feel differently about anything. Your self-worth and self-esteem are a matter between you and your Soul. Your job is to see and experience yourself as the Divine sees you. Your job is to align with this loving force and stand centered in this peace of knowing that you are okay, just as you are right now.

## KNOW THE PURPOSE OF RELATIONSHIPS

When you believe that someone has the power to make or break your mood and control your state of happiness even to the slightest degree, you've in essence made them your God. This is not a spiritual relationship because this other person is not your God. When most people think of a spiritual relationship, they think of

Soul mates and some kind of rare, special, romantic relationship that is in perfect harmony. In this type of relationship, the partner often has a huge amount of God-like power over the other person's happiness and well-being.

A truly spiritual relationship is one that moves you closer to a divine connection with that Spiritual Source within you, a connection with unconditional loving. A spiritual relationship can be any relationship, and it can happen at anytime. It can be a friendship, an acquaintance, a lover, or just a passerby. It can also be an enemy.

Any relationship has the potential to bring you to that experience of feeling connected to your Divine Essence. Any relationship can have the experience of connected Oneness. Any relationship that teaches you and moves you closer to peace and love in some way is a spiritual relationship.

Gandhi said, "Be the change you want to see in the world." Well, for most of my life, I thought if everyone else would change some, then my life would be a lot easier and everyone would be much easier to love. After a string of three broken, painful, romantic relationships in just a few years, I started to wonder what the common denominator was with all these "defective" women I was dating because none of them were able to make me happy, none of them seemed to serve the purpose I thought they would.

After a humbling, exhaustive search, I realized the common denominator wasn't going to be found in them; it was going to be found in me. I realized that it would be a lot easier to change me than to change them. I realized that I couldn't control other people, but I could control how I related to and experienced other people. The world didn't have to change for me to enjoy it; I had to change the way I saw the world and the way I saw everyone in it.

So I started looking at my relationships in a completely different way. I started to seek a higher purpose in these relationships. I started to see that those people who triggered my inner upset were not disguised devils trying to hurt me, but rather angels who were sent to help teach me some lessons about how to love better.

Maybe you have several people in your life who are difficult to deal with, or maybe there is one person who constantly triggers you to upset? It is with these difficult relationships, with these difficult people where you have the opportunity to grow the most. Whatever the challenge or lesson, it is one that you must overcome or learn, or you will be destined to repeat it again and again until you do. Pain means that school is in session.

You may think that you can get rid of or change the person that is creating so much upset inside you, and that will fix things. Getting away from him might help if that is a lesson you need to learn. However, if it's an inner lesson, which it usually is, the Universe will keep sending you different people that trigger the same disturbance in you over and over until you get it right.

Have you noticed how others seem to get involved in the same types of painful relationship situations over and over again? The names may change, but the situations are almost always the same? It's because they haven't learned the lesson. That's what happened to me. I'd get rid of one person that upset me a certain way, and very soon I'd meet another person who would bring up the same things. How is this happening in your life?

A relationship's purpose may be completely different from what you have in mind for that relationship. The conflict between what you want and what the Universe wants for you is where you are most likely to get stuck. You may want someone as a dedicated partner, an employee, a loyal son or daughter, or husband or wife; but the Universe may have a different plan for you and this person. Your ego wants it to be and look a certain way, take a certain form; but your Soul only wants to experience a loving connection.

The Soul doesn't care about the form; it doesn't care how it looks, who he is, short or tall, married or single, wealthy or poor, responsible or irresponsible, friend or lover. It only cares about the loving content of the relationship. Is there a loving connection? That is all it is concerned about.

You're part in all this is to determine what the Universe's intended plan is for you and accept the form, however it shows up. You have to learn to love no matter what that plan and form may be. Imagine feeling love in your heart and connection with everyone while not being affected or unduly concerned about what they are doing, who they are with, or if they are staying or going.

Your relationships will present you with three major lessons: how to love yourself, how to love another, and how to share love. Most relationships will have elements of all three, but some will be obviously more heavily weighted toward the lesson you most need to learn.

## ✦ Lesson 1: Self-Love

You will know your lesson is to love yourself when you are seeking love, wanting attention or approval from someone, and not getting it. How many times have you felt like you were giving and getting nothing in return, wanting but being denied?

When this type of situation occurs, you may feel many things: *betrayed, neglected, belittled, depleted, diminished, disregarded, envious, jealous, helpless, victimized, less than, inadequate, insecure, unsafe, needy, powerless, wounded, wrong, unlovable.* If you feel any of these, there is a lesson for you in how to better talk to yourself and think about yourself.

It may not matter how much others really love and care for you; you may not be able to experience that because you don't hold enough love for yourself in that moment. If you are constantly presented with any of these feelings, the higher purpose of these experiences is to heal the part of you that doesn't think you are enough.

If you find yourself always doing for others with little time for yourself, there is a lesson here for you. If you feel you must do for others in order to be loved, there is a lesson. If you believe the love you need comes from others, there is a lesson.

It can start by identifying what it is you are needing or think you are needing from someone else and not getting. Your thoughts can give you a lot of clues. If you think you're being abandoned, for example, how are you abandoning yourself? If you think you've being betrayed, how are you betraying yourself? If you think you're not respected, how are you disrespecting yourself? Whatever you're not getting from another is what you are not giving to yourself in some way.

It is on this level that you can begin to know how to fill the void. This is where you really need to self-reflect and ask yourself, *How am I not loving myself?* and *What can I do to feel complete?*

When you get an answer from your Soul, you go with it.

For many years, I thought I couldn't feel whole and complete without the love of someone else. I thought that only the "right" person loving me could take away the fear and loneliness. I never believed I could find it on my own within myself until I did.

When you are able to love yourself, you don't care that much about what others say or do. You are not attached to their actions. You don't need them to give you anything to feel okay with yourself. You just feel okay with you because you know deep down you are okay.

When you really want and think you need something from someone else, this is when you most need to focus on you. I often hear people complaining about how they give and give to their partner and get nothing in return. Forget about getting whatever it is from them, and start learning how to give that to yourself. Self-love is the solution. Sure, it's wonderful to receive, but the only thing that is going to fill you to your depths is seeing yourself as the Divine sees you.

Getting another person to love you, proclaim or show their love for you in some way, will only take you so far. If you aren't feeling love for yourself and thinking of yourself from that place, it doesn't matter how much outer affirmation you get. It will never suffice. You must move towards self-affirmation.

Nearly every relationship at some point in time will present you with the opportunity to love yourself more. The majority of the issues you will be presented with in any of your relationships will come back to you and how you are not fully loving yourself. Loving one's self in a consistent way takes constant practice and self-management. When you love yourself, you don't look for it somewhere else, and this takes a lot of pressure off every relationship.

## ✦ Lesson 2: Loving Another

You know your lesson is to love another when you are not accepting him the way he is. Whenever you are attached to someone being a certain way or doing things the way you want, you are not in a loving state. When in this unloving state, you may think, "If only he would change this or that, then all would be great." From this place, you likely feel a level of hostility towards him.

Some of the words associated with this experience are *vengeful, resentful, critical, antagonistic, spiteful, oppressive, judgmental, belittling, hateful, angry, blaming, uncompassionate, unforgiving, argumentative.*

It's easy to love those who are fun and easy to get along with, but those that are difficult show you where your own inner work lies. And some of these people are more challenging than others.

But this is all part of a big test. The better you get at loving other people, the more fulfilling your life becomes; however, there will almost always be someone testing your ability to love. It's like walking up a spiral staircase toward the experience of Heaven—the first step is easy; but as you climb closer and closer to inner peace, the rungs can get harder and harder to step up. Just when you think you've got this unconditional loving thing figured out, the Universe gives you another test in the form of a difficult person, to once again test your ability to find that loving connection. But it's good because it teaches you how to overcome whatever may still be blocking you.

As long as you believe you see something wrong about someone and feel the need to correct it or make them guilty because of it, you will not feel at ease in your heart. You will not feel connected to your Soul.

The challenge is to see whether you can love past someone's difficult personality, behavior, or flaw. It's easy to cut off your flow of love when someone irritates, rejects, annoys, threatens, or scares you. But the test is to see if you can find a way to love him.

You may think someone is a real ass, and others may agree with you. There may be a worldwide consensus that this particular annoying, aggravating person is a real ass. And you may feel completely justified in disliking this person.

However, if you are upset, it's the lack of unconditional acceptance you carry inside you that is causing you the problem. It's not he that is holding your loving feelings hostage. It is you. And you can change that inside yourself, and the other person doesn't need to do or change anything. It's a shift that you make completely within yourself.

It is important to recognize that a relationship is within you. Remember, "A relationship is how you hold another inside of yourself." It is your thoughts about someone that determine whether you experience peace or upset. How someone else behaves or what they think about you is really irrelevant to how you choose to experience the relationship.

Of course it is wonderful to have a free flowing exchange of love with another, but it is not absolutely required that the other person participate in order for you to have a loving experience of them. If you are thinking and feeling connected to love inside of you, it doesn't matter what the other person is doing.

So how do you love someone you don't even like? Love has nothing to do with compatibility. How someone fits into your life-style or whether or not it is good to have this person in your daily life is a separate issue. A friend said to me while I was trying to break up with a very difficult woman, "You may have to throw her out of your apartment, but you don't throw her out of your heart!"

Oftentimes, people are unbearable or even unsafe to be around; you have to remove them from your physical world. This doesn't mean you can't find love for them. You can lovingly punish a child; you can lovingly put someone in prison; you can lovingly divorce someone. Just because you put someone out of your life—discipline, correct, or change the form of the relationship, doesn't mean you should cut off your love inside you.

We've been conditioned to think that if we don't like or agree with someone, we should not love them. We've been taught that if a romantic relationship doesn't work out, we shouldn't love this person anymore.

This is a big mistake and spiritually disastrous to your inner peace. Just because the form of the relationship didn't work doesn't mean you can't still love and care for him with the relationship taking a different form. In fact, if you try to stop loving someone, you will hurt even more. The way to heal a broken relationship is to find more love for that person, not less. It is really quite simple: Loving always heals you; resisting love always hurts you.

I once had a young romance with a woman I deeply loved, or thought I did. As time went on, we eventually fought because she was showing interest in another guy. I thought if I broke up with her and cut off any love I felt for her that I could save myself from more jealousy and pain. I was wrong. The more I judged her, tried to hate her, tried to make her wrong, the more hurt I felt.

Finally, I realized that if I could love her more, accept her more, bless her, and let her be on her own path, although a different one from mine, I would be at peace. So that's what I did. I loved her more and let go of my attachment to what I wanted and let her be who she was.

Now, we are able to still be friends. St. Mother Teresa once said, "I've found the great paradox: If I love until it hurts, there is only more love." This is the goal, to love through the hurt, past the hurt, so much so that eventually only love and peace are filling your heart. I know this sounds radical. It is, and it works.

It's easy to think that the spiritual path to loving another means accepting whatever someone does and bypassing or ignoring their dysfunction. On one level, it certainly does. However, loving someone doesn't mean accepting or subjecting yourself to any kind of physical, spiritual, mental, or emotional harm.

Loving another without condition does not mean loving another without boundaries. Loving someone doesn't mean sacrificing your own well-being. When you are aligned with true loving, you aren't sacrificing yourself for another and another is not sacrificing himself for you. It's a mutually beneficial experience.

Loving another unconditionally is about loving the innocent Spiritual Essence of him. It is seeing and experiencing this other person as a lovable Soul, perhaps in some cases, trapped inside a wounded, disagreeable, even dangerous body. This person may seem to have nothing to offer you and may even be hurtful to have around. This person may be a major pain; but in order for you to feel centered inside yourself, you must find something worth blessing inside of him.

The poet Henry Wadsworth Longfellow said, "If we could read the secret history of our enemies, we should find in each person's life sorrow and suffering enough to disarm all hostility." When you return yourself to peace through loving thoughts, you become realigned with Soul-consciousness. Returning to love doesn't necessarily mean returning to the ugly relationship.

The people you find to be most difficult and most unlovable are exactly the ones who usually need it the most. This person may be incapable of expressing himself in a loving, caring, sensitive way; but that doesn't mean you have to be that way. He may not be capable of receiving your love or giving love; but that doesn't mean you shouldn't give it. Buddha taught, "Carrying resentment is like holding a hot coal. Waiting to throw it at somebody; you are the one who gets burned."

By not loving another, you are separating from your Soul and only hurting yourself. By loving another, you bring love to yourself. You bring the experience of Soul-connectedness to your heart. This is why Jesus taught, "Love your enemies." In order to do this, you may have to get over your pride, drop your ego's need to be right, and humble yourself instead. The ability to love someone who spites you or rejects you takes a lot of spiritual strength. Make the only goal love, and the Universe will help you find the way.

The one sure way to know if your ability to love another is being tested—ask yourself, *Am I loving and accepting this person without condition, or am I wanting him to change so I can love him?*

### ✦ Lesson 3: Sharing Love

If you've ever felt "in love" where you were blissfully excited about someone and the potential for the future, you know how wonderful the world can suddenly look. Being "in love" is the temporary taste of the spiritually loving experience. Although I distinguish a stark contrast between being "in love" and being loving, the physical "high" is much the same.

The experience of love makes you see everything and everyone in a beautifully harmonious way. The problem is, this experience often fades away, the relationship changes, and you walk away not knowing what it was exactly that made you feel so wonderful. Most people believe and will tell you it was the other person who made you feel so good, that it was their presence that brought this loving connection.

It wasn't their presence. It was you, dropping your judgmental thoughts about him and yourself. It was you, letting down your guard and seeing someone as beautiful, as well as seeing yourself as beautiful.

Love occurs when you see and experience their perfection as well as your own. Love is a spiritual experience because you feel connected to something bigger than yourself. It shows you what the potential is for more than just one special relationship—it is for all your relationships. When you are involved in a shared loving experience with only one other, this is an opportunity to learn how you can expand this experience into other relationships. And I'm not talking about sex. I'm talking about the spiritual connection you're having. How can you expand that?

You've been taught to think that you only fall in love with another person, but you are also falling in love with yourself at the same time. The beauty you see in someone else is reflected back to you. This is how Soulful love works; you can't connect to it and not feel great about yourself. And there is nothing wrong with that. Love fills you and everyone who participates. How wonderful would the world be if you could reproduce this connected feeling with all those around you!

The loving experience is what we all want to share with another all the time. And you can move towards that if you stop looking for someone to give it to you and start realizing that you can have a loving experience with just about anyone. You think you have to find one special person to experience profound love, but you don't.

Love can be experienced with anyone. When you are connected, it doesn't matter who it is, what form the relationship takes, where it's going or if it will last or end. Love is experienced in the moment; it can only be contained as long as you maintain thoughts of appreciation and gratitude for those in front of you.

When you fall "in love," you will typically feel bliss in the beginning and then pain when the relationship changes or dissolves. Wouldn't it be great if you could stay closer to the blissful side without the pain?

The lesson here is to take the skills you've learned that brought you to any loving experience and use these in all your other relationships. By doing this, you will no longer be brought to such a painful place if the relationship changes form or dissolves. When you know how to get yourself back to a loving place, you won't buy into the false belief that some "special person" brought you there. Once you know this truth, you will be able to have much more love in your everyday life.

The spiritual purpose of all relationships is to bring you back to paradise within yourself and to see the world from that place. When love is experienced in this way, it is expansive and contagious. So anytime you feel love, whether it be for a lover, a friend, a pet or whoever, this is a glimpse of the paradise the world could be if you can see everyone this way. This way of loving is the ultimate goal.

# CHAPTER 6

# Be Okay with Being Alone

*The soul that sees beauty may sometimes walk alone.*

—Goethe

Our society has made it shameful and wrong for you to be alone, but it is in your aloneness that you learn how to make a Soulful connection. If you are one who is very uncomfortable being alone with yourself, you have yet to make peace with your inner demons. And until you do, the Soulful connection will remain just out of reach, hiding just beyond the fear.

Not long ago at a coffee shop, I heard a young woman telling her friends about how her boyfriend was a jerk and how they always fought. In her very next breath, she said he needed to hurry up and marry her because she didn't want to be alone the rest of her life.

I about jumped out of my seat to shake her awake. She was ready to commit her life to a relationship that wasn't working because she was afraid of being alone someday in the future. Whether she was truly afraid or just conditioned to avoid being alone, I'll never know. Nevertheless, she was certainly not comfortable with the idea. And this is true of many.

The thought of being alone is one of the greatest fears any of us can have. It can shape and affect our lives in so many ways that we aren't even aware of. I know some who would rather stay home hungry than risk the fear or shame of going out to a restaurant by themselves for a few hours. I know others who are growing physically ill because they've trapped themselves in troublesome, loveless relationships they won't leave; they are too scared of the thought of being alone.

Your ego would prefer you to not talk about this, look at this, or deal with any of it. It would much rather have you focus on finding someone or some distraction to fill the void you feel inside. Your ego mind would rather do anything than have you be alone with yourself; to the ego, there is nothing worse, nothing more horrifying than being separate and alone.

We spend a lot of energy avoiding being alone, yet most of us don't even know the full experience. Most of us have never really been alone with ourselves for any stretch of time. What is it about the thought of being alone that frightens and saddens so many of us so much?

## What It Means to Be Alone

Society reveres togetherness, couplehood, and marriage; yet it pities those alone, single, and unmarried. It glamorizes finding a mate and sympathizes losing one. It celebrates marriage and mourns divorce.

Our culture makes being alone something that is really not all that acceptable. We're taught that being single is being a second-class citizen and just something to tolerate until we find someone. This mindset can be a very unhealthy place to be because life creates many situations where we will be alone.

What society fears, it harshly condemns. And it fears being alone probably more than any other life experience. All around you are people who are scared to death of being by themselves, and their fears have been projected onto you your entire life. I've asked hundreds of people what their greatest fear is, and the most common answers are "being alone" and "being unloved."

Not having love is probably our deepest, darkest fear because too many people have come to equate being alone to being without love. But being alone has nothing to do with being separated from love.

You can love and be loved while you are completely alone. Love transcends the physical world experience, but your ego won't let you believe that. To your ego mind, being alone means you are unlovable and unworthy, plain and simple. Being alone means that something must be wrong with you, that you are uninteresting, unattractive, or damaged is some way; otherwise, you'd have people with you. It says if you were good enough, you wouldn't be by yourself. It tells you that safety and security come from other people. And it tells you that you won't be okay if you're by yourself.

You may not have ever spent more than a few moments truly alone. You may not wholly know the experience. Yet when you are afraid of being alone, your life is not truly your own. This fear can put your life and inner well-being at the mercy of others. You will direct your life in an effort to avoid this alone experience, and it can cost you dearly.

You may even miss your life's true calling, like the young woman in the coffee shop who wants to get married to avoid being alone. If she marries someone out of fear, she may never realize the true experience of love because she's focused on not feeling fear. She may also be stuck in a seriously incompatible partnership that could cause a lot of emotional distress. The nature of fear is to block love from being experienced; and if you live in fear, make choices from fear, love will not be available to you.

The following are some of the common ways that you may be avoiding being alone. Ask yourself honestly, *Are any of these a fit for me now?*

■ Picking relationship partners that you know are not complimentary to your life because you would rather be with someone than be by yourself.

- Attaching yourself or staying too long in unhealthy, unfulfilling relationships that you know in your heart you want to leave.

- Overvaluing the opinions of others and not standing up for yourself in order to not offend others.

- Making your life overbooked, chaotic, busy with daily tasks that never seem to be completed.

- Having an interest, obsession, or addiction (alcohol, drugs, relationships, food, work, sex, etc.) to keep you distracted from being with what you feel inside.

- Being in constant contact (i.e., always on the phone, emailing, texting) with others to fill voids of time in your day.

- Moving from one romantic relationship to another with little time in between.

- Staying stuck in situations, going with the pack, following what others do, not taking risks by yourself.

- Compromising your integrity, doing things you don't want to do so you won't be left out or alone.

When you are not okay being alone, nearly all of your relationship decisions and life choices are unconsciously made in order to not have to face this fear. Your ego mindset will tell you that there is security with another person or other people; but it isn't true, at least not the kind of security that allows you to rest peacefully inside yourself.

You may want to leave a marriage or partnership; but you don't because you fear being insecure, lonely and unhappy. The irony is that you feel insecure, lonely, and unhappy now, while you are in the relationship. You may avoid starting a new relationship because you fear the pain of rejection or loneliness that could happen if it doesn't work out.

Yet these feelings are actually the feelings you feel every day by not making new loving connections with others right now. You may be resigned to numbness, suffering, and what you are used to in your life. You may not even be conscious of it. It's called "being comfortable in your discomfort." You may think you are preserving your life, your lifestyle, your livelihood by staying where you are.

But are you? Or are you really dying a slow death inside? If you are, you know it on some level; you feel it. You've lost your sense of adventure to go to your edge. You've lost your faith that the Universe will take care of you. You've lost touch with the experience of being fully alive.

Instead of embracing our fears, we've become like domesticated animals that are always looking for someone to take care of our needs and to feed us; but it's not food we seek. We're looking for spiritual and emotional sustenance. We've caged ourselves in our so-called safe lives and relationships, yet we're never without this feeling of dread lurking in the background of our consciousness because there is no such thing as real safety in this world. Life is risky and dangerous, but we don't want to embrace this fact. We can be at peace but not until we detach our sense of inner-spiritual safety from the presence of others being around us.

When you are Soul-connected, you have relationships with people because you want to, not because you need to. You don't bring people into your life to feel safe; you feel safe within yourself. This is the ultimate goal: to feel loved and secure within oneself; and it begins by knowing the spiritual cause as to why you feel insecure.

## UNDERSTANDING THE FEAR

Pascal said, "All of humanity's problems stem from man's inability to sit quietly in a room alone." In all its simplicity, Pascal's statement was right—if you can't feel comfortable and at peace being alone with you, how can you expect anyone else to be comfortable with you? And if the rest of the world is also unable to sit with itself, it's no wonder the world has so many relationship problems.

The underlying reason the human being has a hard time sitting quietly in a room alone is he hasn't connected with the Spirit that dwells within. He can't get past his own mind. If he expects others or things outside him to fulfill his needs, he will always be afraid of being alone. The fears, the self-judgment, and the sense of separation is more than most can stand. This is why so many move to addiction. It is a way of escaping the mind, the fear, and the emptiness that come from not being connected.

This fear of being alone goes much deeper into your psyche than the surface fear of being by oneself in an empty room. If you've ever felt alone or lonely in a relationship or in a crowd of people, this experience shows you that loneliness isn't satisfied simply by the presence of other people. There is much more to it.

There is something deeper inside you that feels you don't fit or don't belong. In its shallow state, it's like the feeling of being a stranger at a party you were invited to. The voice of this fear says things like, *I'm all alone. I'm not welcome. No one here loves me. I'm not safe. I'm in trouble.*

This fear in its deeper state can be very dark, *I'm dying* or *I'm going to die,* and can take the form of a panic attack. If you've ever had a panic attack where you felt completely out of control, breathless, isolated, or desperately vulnerable, you know how alone you can feel.

This is the very outer edge of your ego's comfort zone but at the very beginning edge of spiritual connection. This is the area to be challenged and to move through to the peace that dwells just beyond the intense fear.

Some people experience this desperate aloneness after breakups, divorces, job losses, deaths of loved ones, and other pivotal circumstances where deep attachment or dependency has occurred. This is the experience of the spiritual separation we talked about in a previous chapter. When you make someone or something a god of sorts to you, someone you've become dependent upon in some way, you'll be crushed when the situation changes form. You'll feel very afraid to go forward.

This painful fear of being alone correlates psychologically to your fear of dying, but the threat is happening in your psyche and has nothing to do with your body dying. Your body isn't in danger, but your inner mind is freaking out about the idea of being alone. The ego equates being with someone to being alive, and your Soul equates loving someone to being alive. The ego doesn't have a spiritual connection, so being around others is all it has.

If you've experienced some of this, the lesson for you is that you are seeking love and security in all the wrong places. The experience of love comes from inside you. And you can have this loving connection all by yourself. Always remember, finding love is not about finding somebody. Finding love is about finding the connection with Spirit that dwells within you.

A 16th-century Catholic mystic, Saint John of the Cross wrote *A Dark Night of the Soul,* which told of his experience with deep psychic pain, aloneness, lack of faith, and disconnection from God. The title has come to be a common expression used to describe a specific phase of one's spiritual journey towards enlightenment. During the "dark night" experience, life seemingly loses its color; it's Godless, hopeless, loveless, and very lonely. It's a desperate space inside you where you feel deeply separated, disconnected, alone.

This inner place is where most spiritual seekers and seekers of love turn around. This is an inner place where most addicts who are in recovery relapse. This inner place is the bridge across hell that you must cross in order to arrive in Heaven. It's the bridge of fear; but if you can cross it, you'll step into love.

And you cross it by letting go of all your mind's attachments to what and who you think you need to be fulfilled. It's not fun—it's usually very scary and painful, but we all have the opportunity to face this fear and cross the bridge into the unknown at some point in our lives.

For me, my darkest, most fearful "dark night" moments were when I knew the life I had been living was no longer tolerable for me. I knew I couldn't go backward and keep living the way I was because I'd been there and knew it didn't work; but I knew no other way to live. I was stuck at a crossroads with ugliness behind me and the uncertainty of the unknown before me.

At the time, I didn't have anything resembling spiritual faith. I only relied on myself for my answers, and I was out of answers. I felt like I was in a desolate no man's land inside myself. I had never felt more alone, empty, scared, and helpless in my entire life.

Although there were people who loved me, I didn't feel it because I wasn't connected to the Loving Essence inside me. I was disconnected from my Soul. At the darkest moment, I had no trust that my life and relationships would work out for me. I was panicked. I had lost my connection to love. I was a broken man without hope for myself. I was going through the worst hell of my life, and it was all inside me.

As soon as I realized that many others had been there before me, I knew I could get through it. I just needed to find faith and the love in myself. I needed to find connection with my Soul. After a few days of intense fear, I began to get to the other side. What I learned was that it is loving others and myself that brings me to that connection.

Mother Teresa said, "The most terrible poverty is loneliness and the feeling of being unloved." If you are disconnected from your Soul, you will be disconnected from others. You connect with others on a Soul-to-Soul level through unconditional love and acceptance. When you learn and experience connection to your Soul within, you've freed the mind from all self-judgment. When you connect with your Soul, all the fear disappears and only a loving connection is left.

## BEING WITH YOURSELF

All relationships start with you. Peace starts with you, and it starts from the inside. If you are not in a right relationship with yourself, then nothing outside of you will be right either.

There is a difference between being alone *by* yourself and being alone *with* yourself. You may think you are alone a lot, and it's not a big deal; but are you really with yourself? I mean, are you able to be with your thoughts, your feelings, your inner discomfort, your fears, your pain, and not move away from that experience? Can you sit alone with everything that goes on inside you, listening to it, feeling it, and not trying to distract yourself with anything?

Most people have a very difficult time with this. Most people when by themselves will be working, talking on the phone, drinking, drugging, emailing, watching TV, listening to the radio, or involved in something that distracts the mind and emotions. This is not being with yourself. Until you can be fully with yourself, you will always be on the run from that shadowy figure inside your mind that is telling you that you're not quite safe, not quite good enough.

Seeking inner retreat from worldly distraction in order to connect with the spiritual realm has been a practice of sages, shamans, and mystics for millennia. One of the most famous for his solitary quest was Siddhartha Gautama approximately 2500 years ago in India. After sitting alone in meditation for 49 days under the Bodhi tree amid multiple psychic battles with Mara (the Demon of Illusion), he became enlightened as the Buddha.

Five hundred years later in the biblical story, Jesus went alone into the desert for 40 days to be tempted/tested by the devil and to secure His connection with Spirit.

In native shaman culture, the vision quest is a solo ceremony where a man goes into the wilderness and sits in his sacred circle for days awaiting connection with Spirit and a vision to take back to his people.

Another version of this is where a warrior digs his mock burial place, his "death pit" where he will lie—alive, covered up with branches, in total darkness for days on end or until he has made peace with his own mortality.

All of these intentional solo journeys have the same thing in common: going inward into the darkness to face one's inner demons of the mind and seeking the blessing of Spirit's light to get past them. It's the classic hero's journey; yet in most popular romantic stories, it's a brave warrior or knight fighting some dragon or monster to save his village—which is the metaphor for your hero's journey in defeating those dragons and monsters that dwell within you. It's a battle you must fight in order to save your inner village; for if you don't stand to face them, the monsters will forever prey on you and the relationships you've made and brought within your village.

Your life may or may not dictate the need to go into death pits to find what you need, but at some point I'm sure it will dictate the need for you to be alone with yourself. You may not even realize what is going on inside you, you may not know what kind of demons are inside you until you stop long enough to experience them. It doesn't matter so much how you do it: meditation, vision quest, walking in the woods, sitting by a lake, death pits, just being in your room. What matters is, you go within and get to know you. What matters is, you work towards clearing the part of you that fears and judges while connecting to the part of you that loves.

The process of going solo by intention has not been very popu-lar in Western culture, and we're becoming more neurotic and disconnected as a result. The path to enlightened, fulfilling relationships with others is first a solo path that many won't brave. However, if you do, once you've become able to relate well with yourself and the demons inside you, then you will be able to relate well with others and understand the demons they carry inside them.

Situations like a breakup, divorce, death of someone close, loss of a job, moving, and just about anything else that creates a change in what you are used to can bring about feelings of separation and aloneness. This disconnection can be scary and painful. Most often people will say, "You shouldn't be alone at a time like this."

Rarely will you hear someone say, "This is a good time for you to be alone and re-connect with the Spirit that's inside you." In most cases, this is exactly the best thing to do in a time of change.

Being with others and getting support can be very empowering and nurturing; there is certainly a time for that. Yet it can also distract you from being with what's going on inside of you that won't go away on its own.

You may have heard, "The shortest distance between two points is a straight line." Well, the shortest distance between inner unrest and inner peace is an inward line, not an outer line. And there is only room for one on the path inward.

## BEING WITH YOUR THOUGHTS

When you begin to spend time with yourself looking within, you are going to encounter your thoughts. Have you ever stopped and listened to what voices are going on in your head and how busy your mind is with inner commentary?

You have an inner chatterbox of ideas, demands, and often self-criticisms in your head that never seem to shut up. Observing this is a bit like becoming aware that a catchy jingle is stuck playing in your mind over and over again. After a while, these jingles can make you a bit crazy, and so can your unmonitored thoughts.

This is why you have to become intimate with your thoughts. Listen to them, observe them, and be aware of what they are telling you.

We are taught to believe that we have no control over our thoughts, that they just come to us, but this is not true. If I asked you to think about an image of your mother right now, you could do that. So you have control of your thoughts, just maybe not as much as you could.

Your thoughts are very powerful; and if your mind is untrained and unpracticed, they are mostly in control of you. Most people do not practice focusing their thoughts, so their erratic thoughts run them like puppets on a string. It is your thoughts that affect your emotions, and your reactions are what affect the way you relate to situations. Some of your thoughts can lead you into hell; some will lead you into Heaven.

If you have a situation that is upsetting to you and you want to change it, the first thing to do is work on changing the way you think about the situation. Whatever problem you think you have may not be a problem if you change the way you think about it. For example, many years ago, I was fired from a corporate bank job. At the time, I had just begun to learn how changing my thoughts could really change my experience.

The story begins with my boss, who was a very nice, yet very overworked and stressed guy, called me into his office one morning. I could feel he was nervous and uncomfortable. He sat me down and told me he liked me, but I wasn't making the cut; my production as a loan officer was too low, and my services were no longer needed. He was firing me.

I wasn't sure how to react at first. I had never been fired in my life. Within an instant, my ego mind started to go into fearful and judgmental thoughts about myself and my boss. In that moment, in my mind, I started to plan my defense, argue and tell him how it wasn't my fault that my production was low, how the company wasn't doing the marketing, and so on.

Then inspiration came over me. I took a breath and decided to take a new line of thinking about this. Something inside me told me I was okay and had nothing to fear. I suddenly had no desire to defend myself. I realized that this was the Universe's plan for me, and I should go with it. I was instantly at peace, and my focus shifted off of me.

I could see he still had a lot of fear about telling me all this, so I told him I understood, and I couldn't help but agree with him about my performance and that I thought he was probably making the right decision for everyone. I looked him directly in the eyes for a long time, sincerely told him that I really liked him as well, thought he was a good leader, and really appreciated getting to know him.

He nearly started to cry as I was acknowledging him. He didn't know what to do with it. He was expecting something ugly to happen, not to be complimented and appreciated. We made a very strong connection, wished each other well, shook hands, and went our separate ways.

Two days later, a job opportunity showed up for me when I ran into a friend who had just started a new company. This position suited me far better, and I was much happier there for several years.

By changing the way you think about a situation, you can change the situation. You can make a situation ugly or beautiful; it's all a matter of how you decide to think about it. I could have made my getting fired really disconnecting and nasty. I could have fought, argued, threatened, and made a big scene that would have likely put my boss in a place of more fear, which would have escalated his aggression, making it even worse. Instead, we both chose to be loving toward one another even though the business arrangement was not working for either of us.

Most of us have carved chemical grooves through our brains; scientists call them neuropathways. When you are stimulated by a situation, you are most likely to think and react based on your prior way of thinking. Your thoughts follow the old well-worn trails they've followed for years.

However, good thought management is about stopping a destructive thought dead in its tracks and replacing it with one that is more supportive. Taking the spiritual path begins by blazing a new, loving path through your brain. By practicing awareness of what you're thinking, you are able to make a choice about it and redirect those thoughts. Thoughts of fear can be turned into thoughts of love by making a conscious choice to change them.

Seek loving thoughts, and all will fall into place. Practice loving when your old mind path says, "Fighting is appropriate here," and see how things change.

## BEING WITH YOUR EMOTIONS

Being with your joy and happiness is easy. Being with your uncomfortable emotions is one the most difficult, yet most important things you can ever do for yourself. Most people refuse to be fully with their emotions. They are terrified of feeling them.

Sometimes your emotions can be so uncomfortable, painful, and messy that you will do whatever you can to avoid feeling them. This is why so many people are addicted to so many different things. Addictions distract you temporarily from those feelings, but you're just prolonging the experience.

The *Tao Te Ch'ing* asks, "Do you have the patience to wait until your mud settles and the water is clear? Can you remain unmoving till the right action arises by itself?" Most people can't wait until their mud settles. But if you want to find peace, you must sit with your discomfort, your muddy emotions. You cannot return yourself to feelings of joy and happiness when feelings like fear, anger, and sadness are filling you. These feelings must be released first, or they'll block everything you want to feel.

Being with your emotions means fully experiencing them without distraction and is the fastest way to get through them. You may think what you are feeling will never pass and if you let it flow, you will never come through it. But you will and it will pass.

Only by avoiding the feelings do you allow them to linger, torment you, and make you sick. So when you feel angry and want to scream, scream. When you feel sadness and want to cry, cry. It's been my experience that fear and anxiety will meld into sadness and can be cried away.

And don't judge your emotions as good or bad. There are no good or bad emotions. They are just emotions, and we all have them. Judging them only makes you want to avoid the so-called "bad" feelings, and this doesn't work.

When I first learned the benefits of experiencing my emotions and allowing myself to be with them, I didn't hold them back anymore, which proved to be very beneficial to my healing yet very inconvenient at times.

One day I was driving from Santa Barbara to San Francisco by myself. As I drove, feelings of deep sadness and grief kept coming up, so much so that at times I couldn't drive safely; I had to pull over to have a full-blown crying session. After 5-10 minutes, I'd feel better and get back on the road. Then they'd come back up again, and I'd pull over again to cry. I couldn't help it; the feelings came up, and I went with them.

I took advantage of the opportunity to express and expel the emotions while they were near the surface. Otherwise, I knew they would go back inward and make me depressed again. Thirty years of avoiding my feelings had me pretty backed up and depressed, so I had a lot more "pull-overs" from my daily life over the next few months.

I encourage you to give yourself permission to allow yourself to feel everything, whatever it is. Take as many "pull-overs" as you need in life. Once you do, you will feel a release and make room for love to refill that place inside of you. A Jewish proverb says, "What soap is for the body, tears are for the soul." You have to clear out the old to make room for the new.

Feeling very emotional, upset, and confused is okay. It doesn't mean anything about who you are. When you learn to allow your emotions to flow and see them as only temporary, passing experiences, you can relate to yourself and others in a much more graceful way. Don't mind what others may think or say. Don't mind what your own self-judgment says about crying. It doesn't mean you're weak; it means you're real and fully alive.

Know that you are not your emotions, and do not make critical decisions based on your emotional reactions. You may have been taught to follow what you feel, but don't get your emotional feelings confused with your Soulful Essence. When you have a very emotional experience, it is important to remember who you are and that your emotions are only one aspect of your being.

Your emotions are not very sophisticated and certainly not reliable, stable decision-makers. As you've experienced, your emotions can change moment to moment. And some life choices made from emotions cannot be changed as quickly or easily as the emotions come and go. So it is wise to let the emotions settle out before you commit to something based on an emotional high or low. Let your mud settle.

## Going Through the Fire

The theologian and philosopher Paul Tillich said, "Language has created the word 'loneliness' to express the pain of being alone. And it has created the word 'solitude' to express the glory of being alone." The difference in this experience of loneliness and the one of solitude is a matter of whether or not you are connected with the Soul.

Connecting your awareness with Soul is done by intention. It happens through your desire and willingness to allow connection to show up. You seek it, create a space, and ALLOW it. It's not something you can force to happen. It's not something you can demand. It's something that comes when you are willing to surrender your egoic way of thinking and your way of trying to control the situation. You have to give up your will and your way and let Spirit handle the details that you can't.

This is what prayer is about. Praying is the conscious action of opening a channel to your connection with Spirit. You can call it whatever you like—prayer, intention, talking to God—it doesn't matter because the effect is the same. When your heart and mind decide to open up to Spirit's intervention in your life, it's not a matter of when it will happen; it's only a matter of when you wake up to the fact that it's been happening all along. Now you just have to pay attention and follow the Soul's path for you.

Sometimes you must go through a very dark space before you are able to experience the light. That's how it was for me. I had to go through hell first. I had a very strong resistance to believing in any idea of a Spiritual Source for a long time. But at one point, I was in so much pain from years of stuffing away my emotions that I thought that dying might feel better than this. I said to myself, *What can I lose at this point? I can't feel worse than this.*

As I rolled around on the floor of my apartment off and on for two days, alone in my inner darkness, crying, shaking with fear, I realized that I was at the deepest point of my pain. I had never felt this much emotional pain in my life, and I realized I wasn't dying. The realization that I could feel this much hurt and still be alive was quite a revelation. My ego was dying to my old way of being— that's where all the pain was coming from—but my Soul wasn't. My

Soul was expanding through the darkness.

As I was clawing around in the emptiness, I related my experience to what I recalled of a Bible verse I learned as a child in parochial school, "As I walk through the valley of the shadow of death, I will fear no evil for Thou art with me." I knew I was in my valley of the shadow of my death, but I feared everything. "Thou" was not with me, at least not to my awareness.

I guess I had to cry and panic myself out first. I kept seeking, and peace eventually showed up. I didn't see God or anyone; I just felt deep peace and a presence of connecting energy with everything and everyone. I felt free for the first time in many, many years. I knew how to experience love from that point on.

Upon looking back at this experience, I know I had to keep going into my fear and pain to get to the other side of the valley of the shadow of death. I knew I had to do it by myself, with myself, and that there was truly no other way for me. The hole of emptiness I felt for years was never filled by other people or other things. It was filled by the connection with the Soul that happened in my aloneness.

*The Course in Miracles* teaches, "If you knew who always walked beside you on this path you have chosen, you could never experience fear or doubt again." Isn't this what we all are really seeking? To feel peace and never know fear or doubt again? This is the security we seek in our relationships with others, but this security isn't found there.

When you are able to make the spiritual connection, you will realize inside yourself that even when you are by yourself, you are not truly alone. When you remind yourself that it is the Soul within you that you are really wanting to connect with, all your other worldly desires lose their importance. Once you've made the connection with the Soul inside you, you will be able to connect with the Soul in others, and the world will never look the same again.

# Choose Inner Experience over Outer Appearance

*It is amazing how complete is the delusion
that beauty is goodness.*

—Leo Tolstoy

*P*reconceived ideas of how you think relationships should be and look are holding you back from experiencing real connection in your relationships.

Fifteen years ago I said to a friend, "Wouldn't it be nice to have a normal relationship with a normal person?" This was shortly after a breakup in a romantic relationship that didn't turn out the way I had hoped. At that time, I was thinking everyone else's relationships were working great, but only mine were messed up.

I saw seemingly happy people getting married, buying homes, having kids, and living the relationship dream. I had an image of a "normal relationship" being a Utopic, healthy, fulfilling relationship where everything worked according to plan, where everyone was happy, considerate, and loving toward one another. That's what I thought everyone else had; that's what it looked like everyone else had.

However, as time moved on and I became more aware, I began to see that the "normal" relationship wasn't the normal I thought it was. And the "normal" person was also an illusion. I noticed that one by one, my married friends' relationships started to crumble. Divorce became the thing to do, just as marriage had been years before. The inner issues and inner struggles that once were hidden behind a façade of happiness were now bleeding through like old rust under new paint.

The more I looked around, the more I could see that the "normal" I aspired to wasn't what I had thought it was. Those I had thought were more "normal," and thus better off than I, were really no better off. They just disguised it well.

Of course, there are those who do have very healthy, fulfilling, highly functional relationships; but those are more the exception than the rule. Those are really the abnormal relationships.

By definition, normal means standard or typical. But the standard or typical relationship in our society is fraught with all kinds of problems, disconnections, addictions, and dysfunction. Even the ones that look perfect have skeletons lurking in the closet. If you believe you might be a bit dysfunctional, or your relationship is dysfunctional, or your family and friends are dysfunctional, I may have good news for you. You're normal!

Having complicated and difficult relationships where neither person is very satisfied is what is normal these days. So seeking normal as your goal probably isn't setting your goal high enough, and it's not going to be satisfying.

Extraordinary would be more like it. A Soul-connected relationship is an extraordinary relationship.

However, in order to have extraordinary relationship experiences, you may have to rid yourself of some of the images you carry about how people and situations are supposed to play out. You have to wake up to the truth in yourself and in the world around you. You have to let go of preconceived ideas and societal prescriptions. You have to be a witness to what is real on your own terms.

The four common ways you can keep your relationships stuck in mediocrity or something less than Soulful are by seeking form over content, carrying expectations, pursuing a personal agenda, and living in fantasy. When you are able to redirect your focus in these areas, your relationships will transform into more satisfying experiences.

## SEEKING FORM OVER CONTENT

You've been conditioned to believe that if you can achieve a certain form or make the external situation the way you want it, that will give you the internal feeling you are wanting. But that doesn't work. It's often a lot easier to focus on how a relationship looks on the outside and not focus on what really matters on the inside.

You've heard, "You can't judge a book by its cover." Well, many of us live our lives focusing on the cover of our relationships. We're concerned about how it looks to ourselves and the outside world. We become obsessed with trying to make it fit the form of what a "normal," happy, successful couple *should* be and look like when the content inside is often neglected.

Have you ever asked yourself what you think your relationships should look like? Being in a relationship that focuses on form can be like having a beautiful chair that's so uncomfortable that you don't want to sit in it. It may look incredible; but if you can't enjoy sitting in it, then it's not fully serving its purpose. You may have a relationship that has everything superficially you could ever want, it may look like the perfect situation to others; but if the qualities of love and connection aren't there, then what's the point? A partnership or friendship that doesn't have those qualities is an uncomfortable chair; it hurts to be in it.

We've been programmed to keep up appearances. We've been programmed "to keep up with the Joneses." We've been programmed to create our relationships or marriages to look a certain way. We've been programmed to be concerned about what other people think. We've been taught that if something looks good, it is good. But only ego cares about that.

By now you may have figured out through your own experiences that love doesn't work that way. The Soul doesn't care how anything looks. Love doesn't care how others perceive your relationship. The Soul is only concerned with the inner experience, the content.

I took some time to study what single people want in a mate and found that rarely did anyone say they wanted to experience a deep loving connection as their first priority. Most people responded by identifying some physical form or situation first. Most first responses had to do with what a partner looked like, his profession, level of education, where he lived, whether he was single, divorced, with kids, and so on. All of these forms have a level of importance on the worldly plane, but they have no importance on the spiritual plane and have nothing to do with the experience of connectedness.

However, you've been conditioned to think they do. Your mind has a set of qualifiers and disqualifiers that says things like, *I want to fall in love with and marry someone who is tall, handsome, and rich,* or *I can't see myself with someone who has kids* or *I wouldn't be caught dead with a guy who dresses like that!*

Your ego mind is attached to situations, things, and people taking a certain form. When they don't, your ego mind tells you they aren't good enough or lovable because they don't appear the way you thought they should. This blocks you from experiencing love. Remember, the Soul's goal is not to find someone with certain qualities or certain things. The Soul's goal is to experience love and connection.

If you have goals to be married or to have kids or live a certain lifestyle, that's fine; but it may not be the Universe's plan for you, and you may find yourself deeply disheartened because those things won't deliver you happiness by themselves.

Your ego also tells you that if *your* things aren't in a certain form, then you aren't lovable. This is why you see so many people who drive fancy cars they can't afford and who live above their means. The way they have it set up in their minds is, *If I have the good stuff other people desire, then it makes me good and desirable.* The truth is, no matter what stuff you have, no matter what level of social status you attain, no matter how perfectly the forms of your life look, they will not give you the experience of love and peace. Ever!

I have a friend in Los Angeles who just bought a beautiful, expensive luxury car that she can't afford. When I asked her why she bought that particular make and model, she said, "The car represents who I am." She also insists on only dating men over six feet tall who appear to have good careers. She believes that if her life looks fulfilled, it will be fulfilled.

But it's not working. She has the form, and she's still not experiencing the love and peace she hoped it would give her. Because it can't.

How many couples have you known who looked like their marriages were perfect, seemingly had everything going right and then the next thing you know, they are getting divorced? I've seen it happen many times. What something *looks like* isn't what something *is.*

The celebrity media shows happy couples as those who are cute, fashionable, have nice homes, glamorous lifestyles, and successful careers. But this *form* doesn't make for happy, successful, love-filled *content.* Just because a couple appears to have everything they could ever want or are "cute together" from an outsider's view doesn't mean they have what their Souls crave on the inside. This is often demonstrated by many short-lived celebrity marriages, drug and alcohol addictions, and in some cases suicide. In the instance of suicide or addiction, the public always says, "How could he do this to himself? He is good-looking, has money, a great career—he has everything going for him."

The answer is, form doesn't supply content, and the Soul only wants content.

Many relationship experts have written scores of books about how to achieve a form for your relationships: how to get a boyfriend, how to get someone to the marriage altar, how to capture a wealthy husband, how to keep your failing marriage together, how to get a better body to get a better man, and on and on. The problem with all of these is the belief that achieving or maintaining form will give you what you really want.

It won't. Just because you get someone to marry you doesn't mean you will experience love in that relationship. Just because you keep your unhappy marriage from ending in divorce doesn't mean you're going be fulfilled because the marriage stays in form. Form doesn't equal content, no matter how much you hope it will.

The outer form has absolutely nothing to do with whether or not you're feeling love and peace inside. An example of this is when a bride spends enormous amounts of time, energy, and money making her wedding event flawless, yet all the while her relationship with her fiancé is crumbling apart at the seams.

Instead of spending time to support and grow the relationship, she spends time to make it look perfect to the world through a beautiful, fairy-tale wedding ceremony. It's a mindset that thinks, *I can control how everything looks, and that will make it all fine.* A flawless wedding ceremony and a beautiful dress don't make for a flawless and beautiful marriage; only unconditional love can do that. But people do this kind of thing all the time, and in a million ways.

My mother used to spend days exhaustively striving to create a beautiful Christmas for our family. She'd set up the tree, decorate the house, send out cards, buy gifts, prepare turkeys, bake cookies and pies, dress up, and so on. She unconsciously believed that if she made everything look perfect on the outside that it would become a magical, happy occasion like perfect holidays are supposed to be. She thought by setting up the proper form that it would deliver the desired content, but it never worked. Not once.

Something disturbing always happened—a fight between family members would break out, or someone would get drunk and insulting, or somebody didn't like their gift. Whatever it was, the magic she hoped for always disappeared into disappointment. We all have had to learn the hard way that decorative place settings at the table don't make for an enjoyable, loving meal together. Form doesn't give us content.

Another problem with seeking form over content is although you may achieve the form, you can't control it for very long. You can't make a relationship's form stay a certain way. Everything of this earth is temporary and always in a state of change. So whatever form you achieve, it certainly will not stay in that form. It is natural that it will change.

Your attitude with relationships must be flexible because relationships are always changing. Instead of working to make the relationship look like you think it should, it's better to focus on making the inner experience something you can always enjoy, no matter what form it takes. If your focus is always on love and peace, you won't care about form.

## CARRYING EXPECTATIONS

When it comes to relationships, there is a new definition for the word expectation, and it is premature resentment. If you expect someone to be a certain way, perform a certain way, or look a certain way, it won't be long before you feel angry or hurt. Because at some point, he is not likely going to meet your expectations.

Having *any* expectations is setting yourself up for inner upset.

Although we've been taught that you should have expectations of people and that you should trust them to live up to your expectations, it often doesn't go as planned because people have ideas of their own and circumstances change all the time.

If you have an expectation of another, and he isn't aware of it, look out! You're almost surely going to be disappointed. When someone doesn't know what you expect, you are setting up both him and your relationship for failure. How can people meet your expectations, even if they want to, when they don't know what your expectations are? Just because your mind is attuned to a certain idea or need you have doesn't mean someone else's is. Never expect someone to know what you want or what you're thinking.

If you expect someone to express love to you or treat you a certain way, and they don't perform to your expectations, you are likely going to feel rejected and hurt. And it's likely going to happen to you all the time, over and over again, until you learn to let go of those expectations. You really can't change someone so they behave the way you expect them to. Telling someone what you expect can definitely help, but you're still likely to be disappointed at some point.

The other problem with holding an expectation is, many people express their love in a way that may be different from what you're used to or how you express love. For example, some fathers express love by giving money and gifts to their children. Maybe they're scared to express themselves another way; nevertheless, this is what some do. But if the children are expecting verbal affirmation or physical affection, they may never get that. It doesn't mean the father doesn't love his children; it just means their expectations aren't matched with his expressions.

You may live out your life thinking you haven't been loved by a parent unless you figure out how to see he is expressing love in the best way he can. You have to take a different perspective.

Another one of the most common ways you can set yourself up for frustration is in expecting people to play a role according to your standards. For example, a boyfriend has a role, and that changes when he becomes a fiancé, and then it changes again when he becomes a husband, and then it changes again if he becomes a father, and again if he becomes an ex-husband.

For each of these roles, you have a different set of behavioral expectations. You may not expect a boyfriend or girlfriend to live with you in the same house while you're casually dating, but I imagine you would be quite disappointed if your new husband or new wife decided not to move in with you after the wedding. But why would you expect him or her to move in? Because you've been taught to have expectations concerning how relationships work and look. You've been taught that married people are supposed to live together, that it is "normal," and that's what "normal" married people do. But life really doesn't work out the way most expect. I know several happily married couples that credit their relationship success to living apart.

You've been programmed to expect people to behave a certain way according to their particular role or title. And if they don't, they're playing their role wrong; and this is threatening to your ingrained ideals. But a lot of people will never play the role they are in according to your, my, or anyone else's standard or idea of that role.

This is where you must let go of your expectations and find peace inside yourself regardless of how others are showing up. This is where you must begin to think out of the box and realize that you and those you love may need to relate differently to make the relationship work.

One of the biggest, most crushing disappointments in my life was realizing that my father wasn't the flawless, superhuman, invulnerable man I had always seen him as when I was a child. For many years, I had always expected him to have all the right answers and always make the right decisions. Then one day, to my shock, he didn't.

At first, I was very angry at him. For a while, I felt hatred towards him because he wasn't living up to the person I expected him to be. He was letting me down by not playing his role the way I knew it should be played. I made it his fault for destroying the image I had held for him. This scared me because I wasn't sure I could love him in this new role. I wanted to love him, but he was letting me down in a big way.

But it really wasn't his fault. It was my own. I had created the image and set the expectations, and he never had agreed to fulfill any of them. I had to confront my own ability to love unconditionally and accept that he and the situation were different. When I finally accepted that he was human, that he was just a man trying to do his best to navigate through his own often painful and difficult life, I found compassion and a much deeper love for him. I also found more peace within myself.

Alexander Pope said, "Blessed is the man who expects nothing, for he will never be disappointed." Not expecting is a skill of Soulful enlightenment. By not expecting, you open yourself up for anything and everything to happen. By not expecting things to be your way, you turn the function of the Universe over to the Universe and surrender your illusion of control.

By not carrying expectations, you are not attached to your particular outcome. There is room for Spirit's intervention; there is room for something better. Not expecting anything makes you open for everything, and this is where the peace shows up.

## MAKING AGENDAS

Where an expectation is something you await with a high level of certainty, an agenda is a plan, a schedule that you are working on and wanting to happen. An agenda is a plan you have that is self-indulgent. It's generally without thought or concern for another's well-being or interest. A lot of us carry agendas in our relationships, and we aren't consciously aware of them.

When you have an agenda, you are not likely to experience love because the relationship is one-sided, disrespectful, and unconscious. And your Soul won't let you get away with it forever. Here are some examples of agendas people commonly have:

- Pursuing a mate in order to be financially secure.

- Putting relationships on a timeline.

- Befriending someone in order to better a work or social position.

- Acquiring a "trophy spouse" to make you look good.

- Securing a spouse in order for you to have children.

- Seeking or forcing a commitment from someone so you feel emotionally secure.

- Marrying an incompatible partner in order to obtain a certain lifestyle.

- Staying in an unhappy relationship or marriage to maintain a certain lifestyle.

And there are many others. Any desire you have that uses another person as a means to get what you want or to keep you comfortable is an agenda. We all have them, but it's important that we are aware of them because they will ultimately not bring us the connection we really desire for real happiness.

In order to fulfill most agendas, you have to sacrifice something; and it's usually your inner peace. You generally have to sell your Soul to the devil to obtain or achieve your goal. If you are in or enter any relationship thinking, *What's going to be in it for me?* or *What can this person offer me?* or *I have to stay or I'll lose this nice stuff,* you are neglecting your Soul and are going to suffer consequences.

The consequences often show up as inner distress, separation, fear, depression, and guilt. Achieving superficial agendas will not supply you with what you really need, no matter how much your ego mind tries to convince you that it will.

Many people seek financial or emotional security or some kind of partner permanence as their agenda in their relationships; many people believe marriage will offer this. But there is nothing permanent in the impermanent world. Everything is temporary. The permanence of love through something like marriage is an illusion. Real love cannot be secured by achieving any outer agenda. Marriage doesn't secure love; someone's commitment to always be with you doesn't secure love either. There are many married couples that have been together for decades who share no love for one another, and their Soul's are wilting away like dying flowers.

The ego can be very tricky with you here because it wants to own or show some external proof that a relationship is valuable, that you are valuable. Seeking this proof or false sense of security can really distract your mind from what is important, which is simply experiencing love in the moment.

Something I hear people say that reflects this is, "We really love each other, but the relationship is not working out." If you love each other, the relationship is working out perfectly on the most important level. However, the way you have it set up in your ego mind, your agenda and desired structure for the relationship may not be. The external situation not going as planned has nothing to do with experiencing love between you.

If you ever find yourself thinking that love isn't enough for you, you aren't really loving enough. Don't believe that achieving external goals will bring you happiness. Don't let your mind be focused on achieving some mark of relationship success or something that seems to give your relationship tangible, material meaning.

The trick here is to let go of your agenda, and love and accept another whether things go as you've planned or not. In other words, lose your plan!

If you want to have an agenda and set goals, make those goals love, connection, inner peace, and happiness. And work towards achieving those. If you have a loving connection, you have all the meaning that matters. If you don't, work on that. Find that. Be content with that connected experience. That is all you really need.

## LIVING IN FANTASY

When it comes to relationships looking and being a certain way, all roads lead to right here: your fantasies. Your expectations, your agendas, and the forms you think relationships should take are all part of your mind's fantasy. We talked briefly about how we fantasize our romantic relationships in Chapter 4, but it deserves more discussion because it can be a hugely detrimental factor that can affect all of your relationships.

Fantasy is simply an illusion of the mind. It's your imagination of a future event overlaying your present-moment reality. It's about visualizing something that isn't there or a situation that hasn't happened yet. Two types of fantasies can keep you from experiencing love. The first is the negative future fantasy, and the second is delusional optimism.

### ✦ The Pessimistic Future Fantasy

One day while I was in gym class in junior high, one of the guys on the football team that I thought didn't like me said, "Hey, Biles, meet me outside the gym after class!"

My first thought (my projection) was he wanted to fight me.

So for the next 30 minutes, all I could think about was fighting this guy, what I was going to do, how it would go down, and if I should hide out or punch first. I had myself all worked up. By the time the class bell rang, I was exhausted but ready and expecting a fight. I stepped outside onto the yard between the buildings and got myself into my best fighting position.

He walked right up to my face and said, "Hey, I didn't want to talk in front of everybody, but I'm having a party on Friday. You want to come?"

All of that wasted energy! All the anxiety and buildup for something completely different from what I had imagined! It turned out that we never once threw a punch at each other and began a friendship that lasted through high school. All of my thoughts about him and his not liking me were all made up in my head. They were all negative future fantasies. Ironically, later he told me he was scared of me and thought I didn't like him; that was his negative fantasy.

What creates nearly all fear in you is fantasy about a future event going poorly for you, like my imagined fight. If you observe your thoughts the next time you feel anxious, you will be manufacturing something in your head. There is an acronym that may help you remember this next time you're feeling anxious: F.E.A.R., or Future Events Appearing Real. I also like what Mark Twain said, "I am an old man and have known a great many troubles, some of which came true."

Fear is really quite irrational in most circumstances but nevertheless very destructive to inner peace. Maybe you get caught in obsessing about all the possible things that can go wrong in your life. I was taught to "prepare for the worst and hope for the best;" so I always imagined the worst, completely forgetting about the best things that could happen. The best thoughts rarely crossed my mind.

By thinking like this, the experience was like watching a scary movie scene playing over and over inside my mind. It wouldn't take long before I'd have myself really stressed out. I'd get myself all worked up, scared, with adrenaline pumping before anything real ever happened. Some of the ways you may create negative future fantasies in your own head are imagining:

■ A situation you want to happen not happening at all or going poorly for you.

■ Another person having a hostile reaction to information you supply him/her.

■ You are going to fail, go broke, become ill, or die soon.

■ You will be rejected by another or others.

■ You will feel pain.

It's really important to be aware of your negative future fantasies and know that other people create them as well. It's something nearly everyone does regularly. And it's not a healthy or safe way for anyone to show up. When you've been fantasizing about a situation going poorly, you tend to have your defenses up and ready. It's like having your nervous, shaky finger on the trigger of a loaded gun, ready to fire at someone.

It's just not a good energy to bring to your relationships. This is how wars get started around the world, with fear meeting fear.

Even if you show up calm and peaceful, like my school friend inviting me to a party, someone else may show up, like I did, ready for a fight at the drop of a hat. So you have to be ready to neutralize and relate to someone else's fearful fantasies at times. Understanding that other people create fantasies and illusions in their heads just like you do will help you relate to those sensitive situations when they come up. It's always wise to never underestimate the influence of a fear-based fantasy in another.

When you find your mind going into negative fantasy, stop and remind yourself that you don't know the outcome of any future event. Just because your renegade mind has chosen an outcome doesn't mean that will be the outcome.

If you must fantasize, it makes no sense for you to be a loser in your own fantasy. You might as well fantasize yourself to be a winner. At least you'll feel more peaceful inside while you're awaiting reality to show up.

### ✦ Delusional Optimism

This fantasy is about enthusiastically clinging to an illusion when all the experiential evidence is contrary to it. It's what some say is "hope over experience." This kind of fantasy commonly shows up in the beginning of romantic-type relationships, but it occurs in all relationships.

The romantic story goes something like this: You meet someone who gets your heart pumping. You may immediately start to imagine what he's like and what it would be like to be with him. Your thoughts get carried away with images of a first date, how he will love you, building a relationship, going on vacations together, him meeting your family, wonderful sex, getting married, having kids, living happily ever after. Your mind has created this entire life, and you hardly even know the guy.

This is a delusional fantasy; the experiential evidence you have doesn't justify the dramatic illusions in your head. If you add some expectations to this relationship, it will really be doomed to disaster. If you're prone to thinking like this, rein it back in or who knows where you may end up.

A young, recently married woman came in to see me about her marital problems. She said to me, "He wasn't the man I married." Upon further investigation, she realized that he didn't change; she just never really knew who he was because she had made up a lot of who he was in her head. She took little pieces of information she had about him that she liked and created an entire love story around it. She chose to ignore the red flags of incompatibility in favor of the fantasy. She had a dream, was ready for it, and wouldn't allow reality to get in the way of her wonderful fantasy.

For many years leading up to their meeting, she had lived with an image of life with her perfect man. Then this fellow happened along with some of the qualities she liked, and the rest got inserted into this image she made for him.

Interestingly enough, we later found out that he had done exactly the same thing with her. They both were seeking the fairy tale of "they got married and lived happily ever after." Because both were so enamored with each other's appearance and charm, they chose to focus on those qualities while completely looking past their many obvious incompatibilities and lifestyle differences. They chose their fantasies instead, and it didn't work.

Living in delusional optimism is very common. Here are some of the ways you may fantasize about your relationships:

- Place qualities and character traits on someone.

- Imagine being loved, bonded, connected, adored by someone.

- Picture amazing experiences and a lifestyle together.

- Visualize loving/romantic encounters in fantastic places.

- Imagine him/her satisfying all your emotional, mental, physical, spiritual needs.

- Believe you and your partner are perfectly compatible and share the same personal interest.

- Visualize sex being passionate, connected, and effortlessly fulfilling.

- Think that you like or love everything about this person, and imagine he/she thinks the same way about you.

- Have future visions of your life together: having a family, growing old.

- Think that someone will change so your fantasy will manifest itself.

In this type of fantasy, everything is perfect and everything goes your way. However, fantasy is fiction, a fact that is easy to forget when you're caught up in a really good one. Oftentimes, when you fall in love with someone, you are really falling in love with the fantasy you have built around this person.

The idea of "love at first sight" is most times based on initial physical-chemical attraction and then further built around a fantasy. It is certainly possible to love someone at first sight, and in my opinion there is nothing ever wrong with loving someone. Loving is always a spiritually sound thing to do.

It's a problem when you love someone based on a fantasy you've created about him. Loving through a fantasy isn't really loving because you're not accepting someone as they are; you are loving an illusion. Loving someone or a relationship based on potential is the same thing. You are not loving what is; you are loving what could be.

Ignoring real experiences and clinging to a fantasy can be really harmful to you. I believe this is one of the main reasons for so much divorce these days. People are in love with the fantasy of what marriage promises. People fall in love with someone's potential and who they could be if only they would change some things. So couples get married and then work really hard at trying to change one another to fit into their fantasies. When they finally surrender and it's over, the death of the fantasy can be very, very painful.

Sometimes the death of a dream is far more painful than any real-life failure.

Death of a fantasy doesn't mean the relationship is over; it just means that you now must step up to the reality and find love with what is right before you now. You have to live in the present. To do this, you can't carry resentment because the other person didn't live up to your dreams and expectations. You can't carry bitterness because your agenda failed to go through. You have to let all that go with the potential tears that come from such a disappointment. Once you've let it all go, you can pick up and love what is left. The best way I've found for achieving this is to live in the present moment.

There is no moment but the present. The past is done, and the future is still to be determined. Even though you are very aware of this fact, it can still be very difficult to keep your mind focused on what's happening right here, right now. Your mind wants to shoot out in all directions, remembering past events and fantasizing about future ones. Don't let it get carried away.

If you want your relationships to improve and you want to remove anxiety, you must practice focusing your mind on the present moment. It's really very simple. When you are with someone, be with them 100%; keep your mind with them. Don't be a multitasker.

The time to experience life is right now in this moment. Don't wait any longer to express your love for someone; don't wait any longer to get out of a situation that no longer serves. Don't wait for things to be different someday. Stop striving to be happy someday.

Many people who are in problematic relationship situations say, "Well, at least there is still hope." Hope is banking on future happiness, which doesn't bring you happiness because the future never arrives. You have to bring your mind back to the present and make choices based on what is immediately before you. Right now, in this moment is where your attention must be.

Peace never comes in the future. Love never comes in the future. They happen in the present moment. Right now is all there is.

Be mindful of every task you take. When you eat, eat and be aware and enjoy it. When you sit, sit and be aware of sitting. Whatever you do, do it with 100% awareness and be with that experience.

Seek the love and joy in the moment! The more you do this, the happier you'll be.

## SET CO-CREATIVE INTENTIONS

If you want to realize your dreams and bring life to your imagination, I've found that setting co-creative intentions works. An intention is a plan or desire that is determined by you. A co-creative intention is a plan or desire that determined by you and Spirit and carried out in unison. It's similar to that of a fantasy, where your imagination becomes a want for your life; but the major difference is you are grounded in reality and not delusional.

Co-creative intention is simply a prayer with energy and action behind it. The biggest difference between fantasy and intention is you aren't attached to the outcome of the intention. You trust that the Universe will provide for you if that is what is meant to be, and you will go with it. It's a very different state of mind. An example of a co-creative intention is something like this:

*My intention is to heal my marriage, create a close connection, live a more deeply loving, romantic life together, with a mutual fullness of heart or something higher for the good of all. I am willing to work and do everything within my ability to create this. I release this intention to the Spiritual Force to direct me and handle the details that I cannot.*

An intention like this gives an energetic message to the Universe to step up and help you realize the fantasy or something higher for the good of all. Now this means that you are not expecting your plan to materialize exactly the way you imagine it; it means you are open to that or something wildly different, trusting that Spirit is making the final decisions on what is best.

Taking this open approach also means you are willing to wait. One of my favorite teachings from *A Course in Miracles* says, "Infinite patience produces immediate results." From this state of patience, there is a deep sense of peace with what is right now as well as very strong faith that the Universe will provide everything you need, someday.

When you set a co-creative intention, you know inside yourself that it doesn't have to happen in order for you to be okay. This is very important because if you approach an intention with a desperate neediness, it is highly unlikely that you will see positive results.

When you set intentions for your relationships, I've found that it's more productive to seek the inner experience than to seek an outer outcome. What this means is instead of seeking form, you seek content.

For example, a lonely woman wants and prays for a man to show up in her life, thinking that he is the solution to her loneliness. Her prayer is answered, and a man shows up; but his presence doesn't satisfy her loneliness and creates other disturbances for her. So she goes back to setting an intention for a different man to show up, all the while not addressing her inner experience of loneliness.

After several men come and go over the years, she decides that another man may not be the solution. She then sets the intention and asks Spirit to heal her lonely heart. A few days later, she gets a call from a local charity that needs volunteers. She shows up, makes friends, helps others, has fun, and her loneliness is now forgotten.

This is commonly how intentions get answered. Seeking the outer outcome often doesn't satisfy the inner need because we often don't know what we need or what is best for us. Just think what would have happened if you got everything you wanted or prayed for as a teenager? I know for myself, I'd probably be dead.

By setting intentions that address correction of your inner experiences, you are much more open to what the Universe provides to you that will give you what your insides ultimately want. By setting the intention of experiencing love and inner peace, it doesn't matter so much what things look like on the outside. What matters is what you experience on the inside.

## CHAPTER 8

# Love Yourself

*You are a perfectly valuable, creative, and worthwhile*
*person simply because you exist, and no amount of*
*triumphs or tribulations can ever change that. Uncondi-*
*tional self-acceptance is the core of a peaceful mind.*

—St. Francis de Sales

*H*ave you ever noticed how some children are full of love for themselves? The other day I was riding my bike through the park and stopped to visit with a friend who was at a barbecue. As we stood and talked, kids were running all around us playing.

One little boy about six years old stopped and asked if I wanted to kick the soccer ball with him.

I told him I would, but I never played much soccer.

He said, "I'll teach you some stuff. I'm one of the best players in the world!"

A bit surprised at his open declaration, I said, "You are?"

He looked me directly in the eye, with complete confidence, without flinching or hesitation, and said, "Yep!"

Within a second, his happy, cute sister stepped up and said, "He is!"

I expressed my gratitude for being in the presence of such greatness, got my soccer lesson, and thought about how amazing it was for these two little ones to be so confident with themselves, but not in a vain or arrogant way. They just knew they were wonderful, yet not to the exclusion of one another. And then I thought how different the world would be if we all thought about ourselves that way and if we could see the wonder in those around us.

However, the adult world operates in a much different way right now. Childhood joyfulness and self-assuredness get squeezed out of us by our teachers telling us things like "Don't be vain," "Don't be so cocky," "Don't be so sure of yourself." Our self-love and self-confidence, in whatever forms they show up, are eventually criticized by others who lack them. The judgmental, critical world starts to take its toll on us, and lots of us lose that inner light we once had within and for ourselves. We start to get the message that our worthiness and greatness are only determined by others' opinions of us. And we start to lose our good opinions of ourselves.

As kids, we don't see differences in each other as a problem; we see differences as something interesting, useful, and special. It's not until someone tells us that being different is a problem that our minds get infected with negativism like this. Then we start wanting to fit in, be accepted, and be loved by others according to their standards. Because we're being judged, we learn to judge others according to this same measure. Most devastatingly, we learn to judge ourselves—and nobody is a harsher critic of us than we are of ourselves.

## How to Not Love Yourself

The ego's aim is to judge others as not good enough by its standards. When it can't find someone else to point the finger at, it points its finger back at you. The ego also wants you to think that your approval and self-worth come from someone else's opinion of you. It tells you that if you do something good, you will be noticed, appreciated, and loved. You think you will be lovable only when others think you are. This is one of the most dangerous beliefs you can hold on to.

The desperate pursuit of approval (love) from another is one of the single, biggest, life-damaging pursuits of any you can have. Looking to others to supply you with the love you are not giving yourself is at the core of nearly every relationship problem. You want love, but you don't realize that the love you're looking for is a love you haven't found for yourself.

In college, I met a woman named Diana. We became close yet platonic friends. She was quite an amazing person. Very beautiful by anyone's standard, Diana was intelligent, athletic, funny, and had a very likable personality. The problem was, she didn't think so. The guys around campus called her "The Doormat" because she let people walk all over her, especially men. Because she was interesting and beautiful, every guy wanted to be with her; but soon after a relationship began, they wanted to escape her.

She wanted to be loved so badly, she would do anything to get love from whoever her current boyfriend might be. She'd conform her schedule to fit his; she'd constantly buy him gifts; she'd do things she really didn't want to do just to appease him. If he liked poker—she liked poker; if he liked football—she liked football; if he lied, treated her poorly, or chased other women—she'd be upset but put up with it as long as she got some crumbs of attention somewhere along the way. She didn't have an identity of her own that she could rely on. She didn't love herself.

A few years after college, she was hospitalized for a drug and alcohol overdose that nearly killed her. Fifteen more years and two divorces later, she started to look at herself. She stopped using drugs and alcohol and began to find out who she was, what she liked, and what really brought satisfaction into her life. She started to live for herself for the first time, and she began to feel at peace.

Like Diana, many of us have also carried those messages that tell us we should sacrifice ourselves for those we love; and a lot of us have misunderstood this to the point of doing harm to ourselves in the process. Somehow, some of us have it wired into our hearts and brains that to love or to be loved by another means neglecting ourselves.

I've heard people say, "Love is making someone else's needs more important than your own." This is a monumental gesture; but it isn't sustainable, isn't true, and it isn't really loving. Love doesn't help one person at the expense of another. Loving someone else doesn't mean not loving yourself. Love is big enough to contain everyone, and it begins by accessing the love you have for yourself.

"You have to love yourself before you can love someone else" is now a fairly common saying in personal growth circles; but the first time I ever heard that, I think I went cross-eyed. When a friend said that to me, at that time in my life, I was clueless as to what that meant. I had never really considered loving myself. I thought, *How do I love myself? What exactly does that mean? How does that work?*

I had assumed I was loving myself; but what I was experiencing wasn't self-love, and my friend could see it. I pretended I knew what he was talking about, but I didn't. Eventually, I started to get it—not so much how to love myself at first, but how I wasn't loving myself. The love I thought I had for myself was completely conditional, which really wasn't love at all. It was easy to confuse my egoic pride for self-love, but there is a huge difference.

Egoic pride usually comes up when you've done something that you think makes you worthy of praise. For many, it's having money or appearing to have money. For some, it's marrying the most eligible bachelor or dating the most beautiful woman. For others, it might be accumulating awards and trophies from sporting events. Egoic pride is about finding a sense of worth based on someone or something outside of you. It's the ego's voice inside that says, *You're good because you got engaged to that successful guy—you won the* *contest—you got the great job—you got a Gucci handbag—*whatever the goal might be.

This is what I did for years. I sought and had beautiful women, money, and material things because I thought it made me good enough. If I could have the things everyone else seemed to want, then I must be "doing it right." I thought it made me somebody others would admire, and I thought I would admire myself. All it did was further inflate my ego, which made me more unstable and didn't help me get what I was really after.

When you tie your identity and worthiness to someone or something outside yourself like I did, your self-worth is conditional upon the whims and impermanence of the world. You're bound to feel empty and afraid inside because your opinion of yourself is tied to circumstances that are always changing. One minute you're thinking, *I'm cool (lovable to myself) because I've got this wonderful new boyfriend.* The next minute you're thinking, *I'm a loser (unlovable to myself) because we broke up, and he's with another woman.*

The ego always tells you you're lovable because of your association with someone else or because you have a certain something. It tells you that you by yourself aren't enough. This is a lie that affects us deeply, and we need to stop believing it if we want to find peace.

I first began to really understand how I wasn't loving myself by realizing how I wasn't taking care of my body. I was in great shape—I looked very fit—but I pushed my body past the point of healthy exertion. I worked long hours, I over-exercised, I partied at night, and I didn't slow down. I was an obsessive overachiever and would not give myself enough time to rest. *Rest is for the weak,* I thought, so I pushed on because I told myself I had to accomplish things. No matter how much I did, it was never enough. My answer to a tired, sluggish body was more and more caffeine.

Eventually, I'd have to stop my frantic pace because I would become ill. Then I'd feel guilty for taking a day off from work. I didn't enjoy working myself really hard, but I couldn't let myself enjoy a day of relaxation—I couldn't win in my mind no matter what I did.

How are you not loving yourself? Have you ever given it much thought? In order to see yourself clearly, you have to step out of your ego mind and into the mind of the Observer. If, in your mind, you back away from your own drama, like a ghost hovering around you, you'll be able to see how you operate.

From the place of your inner Observer, you can watch yourself and your behaviors. When situations come up that are upsetting to you, ask yourself, *Am I truly loving myself right now?* Take a look. I think you'll find that nearly all the relationship issues that upset you will come back to some aspect in which you are not loving yourself enough.

The following is a list of the four main aspects and some of the common ways we neglect to care for ourselves in these areas.

## 1. Physically

Many of us neglect our bodies in a multitude of ways.

We eat too much, or we don't eat enough. We consume foods and substances we wouldn't dare give our pets, but we don't think twice about it when it comes to putting them into our own bodies. We don't get enough rest and push through our fatigue with stimulants like coffee, tea, sugar, drugs, and sodas. We either don't exercise enough, or we exercise to the point of injury; and even that doesn't slow some of us down.

We push ourselves until our bodies eventually react with illness, and then we don't give ourselves time to fully recover before we are back on the job. Exhausted and infectious to others, we push on to work, thinking we have to keep pushing on, no matter what.

Truth is, we don't *have* to do anything! We *choose* to do it. We choose to push ourselves into the ground because some fear inside is driving us. Whether it's too much of something or too little, we all know on some level how we're not taking care of ourselves.

If we treated other people's bodies the way we treat our own, some of us would be thrown in prison. Imagine someone being put in your care, and it is your job to attend to her physical needs. Would you care for this person like you do yourself, or would you do better?

I know countless people who punish themselves daily. Some live on six hours of sleep a night, smoke cigarettes all day, work twelve-hour days, drink six cups of coffee and three sodas, eat only one meal of a burger with fries and a candy bar, rush frantically from place to place with no breaks, and then drink a six pack of beer or a bottle of wine while watching hours of TV before going to bed.

Many of us don't care for ourselves much better than this, and some of us are even harder on ourselves in other ways. If you treated your child in any one of these ways, you would be considered an abusive parent; yet many of us do these kinds of things to ourselves day in and day out. When you're not sure if you're taking loving care of yourself, ask yourself this: *Would I want this for my child, my pet, someone I love?*

## 2. Emotionally

We neglect our emotional well-being just as harshly as we do our bodies at times. We avoid experiencing and expressing our emotions. We hold in our fear, anger, and sadness until we experience depression or other physical ailments. We also suppress our joy and happiness to conform to a semi-stoic world that often feels threatened by any dramatic display of emotion. We avoid telling people about our feelings because we're afraid of being judged, abandoned, or rejected. We don't allow ourselves to be okay with crying and grieving over a loss—whether it is a death, a troubled relationship, a worrisome job, or something else of importance to us.

We drink alcohol and/or take illicit drugs, prescription narcotics, sleeping pills, and antidepressants. We overwork. We overeat. We become hooked on sex, religion, self-help books. We zone out in front of the TV and computer. We chase relationships. In short, we can become obsessed with just about anything or any activity that takes us away from our uncomfortable feelings.

Our culture places rules and constraints on our emotional experiences. It's okay for a man to be angry, but not for a woman. An angry woman is called a bitch. It's okay for a woman to cry, but not a man. A crying man is called a wimp. We're told we shouldn't grieve too long over a relationship breaking up; we should just "Get over it!" In truth, we get over it when we get over it, and it takes however long it needs to take.

We are a society that prefers not to feel or express much of anything. We will do just about anything to avoid feeling our emotions, especially those that are uncomfortable. But we can't get to the pleasurable ones when we carry around a lot of hurt.

Escaping your emotions is not loving yourself. Loving yourself would be not running from an important, integral experience of who you are. Loving yourself is allowing yourself to fully feel everything.

## 3. Mentally

We torture ourselves on the mental level at times with our destructive thoughts and negative fantasies. We constantly think about what we should have done or what we should be doing. We mentally analyze our every move, looking for places we might have made a mistake. And if that isn't enough, we analyze other people's mistakes as well, especially ones made by those close to us. We find fault and place guilt on ourselves and others, maybe not verbally but with our judgmental thoughts. We also allow our minds to be idle and become stuck in a rut.

When we stop pursuing consciousness, growth, and learning, our minds become undisciplined, and negative self-talk begins to take over. We allow our thoughts to fly unbridled through our minds. It can be like having ten TV sets and ten radios on all at the same time inside our heads with no one monitoring the noise level of any of the ten. When our minds go at an accelerated pace, so go our bodies, creating fatigue, anxiety, and separation from peace.

We can submerge our thoughts in both inner and outer conflicts. Our mainstream media is full of hate and controversy. If we allow our minds to be drawn into those fights, which really aren't our fights, we'll make ourselves sick. Conflict is very, very enticing to the ego. It wants to get in there and stir it up and make its point. In truth, all that really happens is that we get stirred up inside. Fear levels increase, and our sense of calm quickly evaporates.

I was once lying on my couch watching the news on TV and occasionally looking out the picture window to my yard. On TV, there were fires, murders, bombings, people fighting about politics, people telling the audience that the world is coming to an end, and so on. As I lay on the couch "relaxing," I began to observe my thoughts moving toward negativity, and I could feel fear coming up inside me.

Then two squirrels darted by my window, chasing each other up and down the trees, having a great time.

In that instant, I woke up to something! There I was looking at two worlds through panes of glass: One was the TV world out there somewhere; the other, the world right outside my window. One world brought me thoughts of fear and upset; the other brought me joy and amusement. One world was full of chaos; the other seemed peaceful.

I saw right then that I had a choice. Which world did I really want to experience? My ego almost wouldn't let me turn off the TV. I wanted to relax, but my ego mind wanted to mix it up with all the hate-based drama. I had to force myself to turn off the TV and move my focus to what was really happening in the world closest to me.

Another way we can torture ourselves is with our negative thoughts and attitudes. We often imagine the worst outcomes for situations when we truly have no idea what will come about. By thinking something is bad or imagining something bad will happen, we experience the toxic emotional energy right now, in the present.

Our bodies react to imagination just as they do to reality; they can't determine the difference because our imaginations are so vivid and so tightly integrated with our nervous system. We are only hurting ourselves and creating internal anxiety when we choose to experience anything from a negative perspective.

You wouldn't encourage a friend to only think negatively about a life situation, but you will allow yourself to drift off into negativity about your own. Fantasizing negatively about the future or allowing your mind to dwell in the unpleasant past is not loving yourself.

## 4. Spiritually

Many of us in modern society do not tend to our spiritual nature. As a result, we rarely experience real connection in our lives; we let ourselves become starved for love and feelings of unity. We crowd ourselves into big cities where nearly all the creations surrounding us are man-made, and we've lost connection with Mother Nature.

Every day, we find ourselves in such a hurry that we fail to connect with those people who are right next to us. We communicate over computer and phone lines, rarely ever getting close to one another, much less developing a deep or intimate caring for those around us.

We often get so caught up with ourselves just trying to survive or achieve that we lose sight of what really matters most to our Souls. When constantly striving toward a goal—whether a relationship, career, or something else, we frequently miss the gifts that the Universe has provided for us right now.

We can get stuck in survival mode. When we do, we forget to enjoy our lives and our friends. We neglect to experience love in our lives right now because we are too busy chasing or avoiding someone or something. We fail to experience ourselves as connected and flowing with the Universe because we are too caught up living like we are the center of it. At the core of all this, we've lost faith.

Some of us may attend a weekly religious service, but we may not experience real connection with authentic peace in our Souls as a result. We go through the motions, doing what we think is spiritual, but we really aren't paying attention or co-creating the flow of love in our lives that we really want.

Only a connection to our loving Soul within will ultimately give us peace. Yet how often do we practice connecting to that place inside ourselves? Many of us have little or no spiritual training and don't believe or know that there is something to gain from it. Others of us have had negative, hurtful experiences with religion and have internally vowed to stay away from any talk or teachings of spirituality because we associate it with judgmental religious teachings.

We have neglected to remove the internal obstacles that keep us from sharing our love with others as well as ourselves. We judge others and ourselves as if we were God and believe we have the power to decide what is right or wrong in this world. As a result of deciding what is wrong in the world, we feel an emptiness inside. In our quest to fill that emptiness, we seek everything outside of ourselves; nothing from outside us can fill the emptiness within.

There are thousands of ways you can deny love for yourself. Here are some that may help you begin to identify more specifically the areas where you are not loving yourself as well as you could:

1. Saying *Yes* to someone or something when you want to say *No.*

2. Procrastinating.

3. Participating in relationships with people who treat you poorly.

4. Over-committing; putting your wants second to others.

5. Eating poorly.

6. Breaking promises to yourself, others.

7. Depriving yourself of adequate sleep, rest, play time.

8. Staying in situations or relationships that no longer serve.

9. Involving yourself emotionally in others' cheap drama, gossip, problems.

10. Enabling, helping others to continue their destructive behavior.

11. Playing small so others don't feel uncomfortable around you.

12. Withholding love, affection from others.

13. Focusing your thoughts negatively on the past or future.

14. Listening to, believing your ego's own negative self-talk.

15. Exposing the body to excessive toxic substances (alcohol, drugs, tobacco, etc.).

16. Not following your own inner voice and direction; acting against your Gut.

17. Avoiding, distracting yourself from facing your inner fears.

18. Holding resentments, grudges against others, yourself.

19. Excessive, irresponsible spending that you can't comfortably afford.

20. Attaching yourself to others or things.

21. Not speaking your truth when it's important to do so.

Now that you have a good idea of what not loving yourself looks like, your mood may be a bit down. Realizing how you're not loving yourself can be a humbling and sometimes a temporarily depressing experience. Knowing what you're doing and not doing to care for yourself is the first step in turning everything around.

So don't beat yourself up about it. That would not be a self-loving act, which we're going to talk about next.

## How to Love Yourself

For most of my life, I never heard anyone say that loving oneself was a good thing. Loving one's self always seemed to be related to vanity or narcissism. Loving one's self was a concept that equated to selfishness, and it wasn't something people liked. I remember a scorned woman's angry comment about an ex-boyfriend and friend of mine: "The only person he's in love with is himself!" And she didn't mean that in a good and healthy way.

The whole idea of self-love has mostly had a negative connotation associated with it, and many of us haven't consciously pursued loving ourselves because of this. It's too bad because self-love is the foundation on which all our other relationships are built. Without a strong, complete love for ourselves, we can never feel at peace with another because our own self-judgment will get in the way.

Loving yourself in theory is simple: It is experiencing and expressing an unconditional appreciation for yourself as you would someone else that you care deeply about.

In practice, self-loving is nurturing the mental, emotional, physical, and spiritual areas of your life. All are included because you cannot neglect one area without that neglect affecting other areas. You cannot departmentalize your being and only care for one or two areas; they are all integrated.

Loving yourself is being aware of and taking care of all areas of your being in the best way you possibly can. It is working in each area to fulfill yourself fully while harmonizing with the Universe's plan for you. It's not about being perfect; it's about being self-loving.

In addition, self-loving is about making peace with the various aspects of yourself that you don't like. It is softening your judgment of yourself. Maybe you don't like something about your appearance. Maybe you have some characteristic that is different from other people's. Maybe there is something about your personality or your performance you don't like. When you focus on something about yourself that you deem a flaw or imperfection, you are separating from loving yourself.

The way to get past this is to acknowledge the part of you that you don't like and make peace with it. You bring it into the light of awareness and decide to gracefully accept it. Once you accept it, an amazing thing happens—it no longer has power over you and becomes an asset. Usually, our personality flaws that cause us problems are really our best qualities that have been over-exaggerated and turned up a bit too high.

Self-love is about living in the present moment. It is accepting who you are and where you are right now. It is not next week when you finish this job or that task. It is not when you lose another few pounds off your midsection. It is not when someone else gives you approval or commits to love you. It is NOW!

Self-love is seeing yourself as perfectly fine, just as you are. It's seeing yourself as a mother sees her child; lovable no matter what. Because you are a creation of the Universe, you were created perfectly. The Universe doesn't make mistakes; you and I do by thinking there is something inherently wrong with us. And because we make these kinds of mistakes, it is you and I who must stop thinking we are imperfect.

It doesn't mean you don't want to grow and evolve; it doesn't mean you don't pursue ridding yourself of the obstacles that inhibit you; it doesn't mean your behavior is perfect. What it means is who you are and where you are right now is how the Universe intended you to be right now. And there is perfection in that. You are perfect, with a perfect Soul, in the perfect place.

Loving one's self is essentially the same thing as loving another. The experience of love is a Catch-22. It doesn't matter to whom your love is directed because love given is the same as love received. If you find someone else lovable, you will in turn find yourself lovable. It's automatic. And if you can see a loving Soul in yourself, you will see the loving Soul in another.

Love works in a circular fashion with no beginning and no end. It flows through you, outward and back in again. On this level, the spiritual level, love is experienced as Oneness. Love does not differentiate between you and another; when love is flowing, it feeds you both.

So when you express or experience unconditional appreciation for another, if you are paying attention, you will notice you have found a loving fullness within yourself as well. When you are feeling good about someone else, notice how good you feel about yourself.

## FOUR STEPS TO EXPERIENCING MORE SELF-LOVE

### 1. Putting Yourself First

Putting yourself first means caring for your own person the way you would someone else that you love. At the spiritual level, your Soul and my Soul are One, connected; we are not separate on this level. It's important to know that you are just as worthy of consideration as another person.

Taking care of yourself is not a selfish, self-centered act to the exclusion or detriment of others. It is inclusive and beneficial to others. It's about connecting to the Soulful place inside you and putting this first, and then loving from this place. The Soul is the divine light that radiates from a place within you, yet also beyond you and outward. There will be times when the Soul may be the only caring voice near. You are deserving of this love and light just as anyone else is.

If you've ever flown on a commercial airline, you've heard the flight attendants safety briefing, "In the event of a loss of cabin pressure, oxygen masks will drop from the overhead compartments. If you're traveling with a child or someone who needs assistance, it is very important that you place the oxygen mask on yourself first and then assist the other person."

This way, you get the oxygen you need, so you can then help others who are in need. It does nobody any good if you pass out while trying to get the mask on someone else first. You both pass out. If you love and care for yourself first, then you are able to love and care for another.

Have you ever felt abandoned? Maybe someone moved away or broke off a relationship with you. This can create a deep sense of fear and loneliness inside. If you once stop looking at the other person and look inside yourself, you'll find that you have somehow abandoned yourself as well. And this is where the deep feelings of fear and loneliness arise.

It's when you no longer take care of yourself and love yourself that you feel abandoned. It's not what they've done to you that hurt so much, it's what you've done to yourself that hurt. When you make someone else responsible for your inner peace and well-being, you've abandoned yourself. When the comings, goings, and behavior of another determine your inner wellness, you've lost touch. You've disconnected from knowing that you are a lovable Soul.

Loving yourself is about not abandoning yourself. It's about sticking by your own side, taking care of your wants and needs without apology. Putting yourself first is about listening to the Soul inside you and following its direction for you. This voice is the voice to follow. For example, if your Soul (also known as your Gut) tells you to exit a relationship, but you are hesitant because you're afraid it might hurt the other person or create a problem, what do you do?

First of all, think—have things ever worked out well when you didn't listen to your Gut's voice? When you don't listen to your Gut, don't you usually end up in some form of hell?

Second, the voice of your Gut knows the bigger picture even if you don't. Your leaving a situation to be true to this voice is what the Universe wants for you and for the other person even if it doesn't look like it in the moment.

If you know you're in a situation that isn't serving your highest good, it isn't serving the other person's highest good either. If your heart isn't in it, you're not in it, and nobody benefits.

If you see the problem and they don't, you're the one that the Universe has designated as the responsible party. It's your job to align the relationship with what's right in your heart. It's your responsibility to make the course corrections. If you don't, you're holding the other person hostage, and you're violating a spiritual order. In other words, align yourself with what your Gut is telling you to do, and let Spirit take care of all the details. Your life will run a lot more smoothly.

Martin Luther King, Jr., said, "The time is always right to do what is right." Follow what your heart tells you even if it appears difficult or creates some initial discomfort. In the end, it will be what's best for all. Attending to your Soul's desire isn't being cruel—it's aligning with what the Universe wants for you and others.

## 2. Saying *No* to What You Don't Want

If you won't say *No* to what you don't want, you can't say *Yes* to what you do. This is the most basic law of the Spiritual Universe in co-manifesting.

Much of your own life is your creation because of your choices. You didn't create the Universe, but you do have a choice in many matters. You have a choice in the people you associate with, and you have a choice in certain directions your life will take. Because our modern lives bring us so many options and so many things to do, it is very easy to be overwhelmed, especially if we try to do everything and accept every opportunity.

The fact is, you can't do everything and be everything to everyone, although the world will tempt you to try at times. The most important truth here is, not everything and everyone is a fit for you. In order to create the experiences you want in life, you must say *No* to the people and activities that aren't a fit.

If you're like many people, you may be reluctant to say *No* to people because you think it will hurt their feelings or they'll be offended. Perhaps it's because you think it's rude or selfish when others tell you *No*. Maybe you think you'll be missing out on something or that you'll create a disconnection. The deeper reason most people are afraid to say *No* to others is because they're afraid it will hurt or destroy a relationship. They're ultimately afraid of a loss of love.

If you have trouble *hearing* and *accepting* another's *No* without feeling hurt or rejected, you're likely going to have a hard time *telling* someone else *No.* We've been conditioned to think *Yes* is the nice, polite, friendly, "loving" thing to say. But sometimes saying *Yes* when you really want to say *No* is not being nice to yourself. It's not Soul-honoring. It's not loving to commit to people and things you're not really into. It's not good for you, and it's not good for them. Would you want someone committing to you if they really didn't want to do it?

In order for me to write this book, I chose to say *No* to just about everyone in my life for a while. If someone asked me to dinner, I would say, "I'd really like to go to dinner with you sometime. Tonight, I've made a commitment to myself to work on writing a book." I said *No* to party invitations, *No* to work and money, *No* to vacations on the beach, and all kinds of other things. I said *No* to everyone except myself and those potential readers I thought could benefit some from what I had to say. It wasn't always easy, but it was the only way I could stay true to what my Soul really wanted me to do.

I said *No,* and the Universe said *Yes* by clearing a path with love and support for me to do what was necessary. Everybody understood because they recognized the power and strength of my intention. Because I phrased my *No* in such a way that I wasn't rejecting them, nobody took it personally, and most people encouraged me onward.

There is a loving way to say *No* to others that doesn't alienate or create separation. When you keep your *No* about you and not about them, it doesn't cut the other person. By not over-committing yourself to people and things that really don't fit for you, it opens up space in your life for all the things that do. If saying *No* is hard for you, practice!

### 3. Asking for What You Do Want

A lot of us pray for what we want, and this is a powerful act. I'm convinced through my own experience that meditation, sending loving prayers, healing energy, and creative thoughts work. The Universe responds in many miraculous ways, but sometimes we just need to give the information to the person in front of us. Sometimes, the simplest solution is the one most overlooked.

I often hear people who come in to see me for counseling saying things like, "I wish my husband was more affectionate with me" or "I want my boyfriend to be more involved with my friends."

My response usually is, "Have you asked him for what you want?"

And then they look at me in astonishment, like my head just fell off, and say, "What if he says *No?*"

"Then you got what you're not getting now; and if he says *Yes*, you're a big winner!"

Being too afraid to ask for what you want is likely to insure you never get it. Others need the information because they can't read your mind. And you need to push through the fear to expand your limitations in order to have the life that Spirit wants you to have.

If by chance you do get a *No* response, peacefully respect it. You want to be a person who honors someone's truth. A lot of people will lie to others because they're afraid of another's dramatic reaction. Don't be offended and take it personally. You certainly don't want to give other people everything they want from you, right? So let it work both ways. You don't want to be one of those people that others are afraid to be honest with. You want to be someone others feel safe speaking their truths with.

This doesn't mean you don't make a new choice based on their response. Getting an honest *No* means you either adjust your wants or you seek them somewhere else. You may even decide to leave a relationship or a job because someone isn't willing to give you what you want.

At least you got to the truth in that you now know and can make an informed choice. Getting a *No* now is better than living your life feeling incomplete and wondering why or relying on the frail legs of hope.

The area of sex is an especially difficult one for some people to ask their partners for what they want. Sexual desires often bring up a lot of insecurities and self-judgment. Many otherwise-happy relationships end because someone is unwilling to speak up. I was talking with a young woman once who said to me, "If he was really right for me, shouldn't he know how to make me happy?"

I told her, "If he loves you, he'll want to know exactly what pleases you. And if you love yourself, you'll tell him."

When you ask for what you want, whatever it is, I encourage you to be specific in your request. You may have to spell it out for someone and be crystal clear about it.

Part of you getting what you want is your responsibility in com-municating it well. Instead of telling the other person what they're doing wrong, tell them what they are doing right and add in your request. It looks something like this: *I really like it when you hold my hand when we walk in public. I feel appreciated. Will you do that more in the future?*

And sometimes, it's best to be straight up and direct: *I want you to hold my hand now.*

Start taking some chances. Ask for what you want, and encourage those around you to ask you for what they want. Once you've done it a few times, it becomes easier, and you'll begin to experience a strong sense of empowerment. Best of all, you'll start to get a lot of what you want.

## 4. Saying *Yes* to the Gifts and Blessings

Life throws all kinds of things at you, but it's up to you which things you catch and which things you let fly on by. I can remember when I was a kid, we'd turn on the garden lights at night. Hungry toads would come hang out by the lights because all the bugs were drawn to the light. There were all different kinds of bugs, but the toads wouldn't eat all of them; they only went for certain bugs and left the others alone. I think some must have tasted better than others. I don't know.

What I do know is that if you turn your light on, you're going to attract all kinds of bugs. If you're a starving or desperate toad, you're going to swallow some bitter ones that will make you sick. But if you're discerning, you'll take your time and pick the really juicy ones out of the bunch. You'll pick the ones that really nourish you.

Some of us have had a hard time saying *Yes* to the really juicy ones. On some level, we think we don't deserve the delicious ones. We try to play small; we keep our lives under the radar of others; we don't want to be noticed; and we live a mediocre, unfulfilled life. We don't want to risk the pain of disappointment again, so we resist saying *Yes* when something or someone wonderful shows up for us. We don't want to get hurt, so we don't move. All the while, we're hurting anyway—we just stay where we are, play it safe, and resist expanding into a more loving life.

Saying *Yes* to a more loving and full life takes some courage. All you need to do is move in the direction you want to go and step toward what you want. One step forward is often all it takes to get the momentum behind you—a *Yes* and one step forward. Good opportunities and good relationships with quality people will show up for you.

If you're not practicing self-love, you may have a tendency to blow it through sabotage. Big lottery winners are classic examples of this. I watched a TV show that chronicled the lives of multi-million-dollar lottery winners who went from rags to riches and back to rags in only a few short years. They were used to a certain low level of lifestyle and problems. When they were quickly elevated out of that, it was more than their psyches could handle without help. So they sabotaged their wealth and, in some cases, blew tens of millions with nothing to show for it. They ended up right back where they started. We are all capable of sabotaging ourselves in certain areas of our lives and staying stuck right where we are now.

By not allowing yourself to sit with the growing pains that come from expanding into something better, your ego finds a way to mess it up. In my past, I've sabotaged great relationships, job opportunities, and all kinds of beautiful situations because I wasn't ready inside myself to accept them. I didn't love myself enough to allow the Universe to bless me with abundance. I didn't know that all I had to do was believe I was worthy, keep saying *Yes* to these great things in my life, and take one more step forward.

Accepting opportunities to share loving and growing experiences is what nourishes you on the deepest level. Saying *Yes* to those people and situations that show up as blessings is an act of self-loving. When people show up to sincerely help you, say *Yes*. It benefits them as well as you.

Tell yourself you are good enough to have a loving, wonderful life. When opportunities show up that will benefit you, push through any resistance you have and accept what is offered. Good things and good people showing up for you is not a fluke or accident. It is something you deserve; it is your natural inheritance.

When you start to focus on the things you want, you're going to see more of those things showing up in your life. If you start opening up to loving people, loving situations, and things that bring joy into your life, you'll start to see much more of that showing up. Listen to your Soul, trust your Gut, and say *Yes* to the life you want.

The following are some of the things you can do for yourself that are Soul-honoring and self-loving:

1. Resting when you are tired.

2. Associating with loving, supportive people.

3. Expressing your love and affection for others.

4. Taking care your body, eating healthfully, sleeping, exercising.

5. Putting your Soul's request first, then attending to others.

6. Staying true to yourself regardless of the influence from others.

7. Pursuing your wants and dreams; honoring others' wants and dreams.

8. Making time for yourself, your own interests, spiritual practice, etc.

9. Saying *Yes* to the gifts and things you want that show up in your life.

10. Keeping your word to yourself and others, living with integrity.

11. Facing down, pushing through your limiting fears and beliefs.

12. Saying *No* to what you don't want and sticking to it.

13. Trusting your intuition, following your inner voice of wisdom.

14. Forgiving yourself for mistakes; forgiving others.

15. Focusing on the present moment.

16. Holding a sense of humor about yourself and your life situations.

17. Living within your financial means.

18. Seeking healthy, joyful situations.

19. Expanding your limits, trying new things, seeking new experiences.

20. Believing in yourself, believing you're worthy.

21. Living life one day at a time, one step at a time.

Authentic empowerment comes when you learn to love yourself without the need for approval from others. It is the knowledge that no one else can give you what you need for your peace and happiness but you. When you love and respect yourself, the world will be more loving and respectful. You will come to know that you cannot be abandoned by another, only by yourself. You realize that although others can enhance your life, they cannot give you what you have not given yourself.

Knowing and living this, your relationships will change dramatically. You will no longer rely on someone else to give you your sense of worthiness because you will already have it. And if you misplace it, it will be only a temporary situation because you will know to seek it from the unlimited well of Spirit within you.

With this attitude, you can move into a place of true giving. You will have a fullness, an abundance of love that you will be able to share with others. Self-love is the foundation for all healthy, connected relationships. With this high level of self-love growing inside you, the dynamics of your relationships will change from "What can they offer me?" to "What can I offer them?"

# Remove "You Should" from Your Vocabulary

*A man should look for what is*
*and not for what he thinks should be.*

—Albert Einstein

disturbing message, one that keeps you from loving and living the life you're meant to have, begins with the words "You should!" For much of your life, you've had people telling you what to think, how to behave, and what path your life "should" go down.

These messages, whether from your parents or other teachers, have become imbedded in your daily thought processes—so much so that you respond to them like they're your own original thoughts when in reality many of them are just old messages from old teachers. Perhaps some of the "You Shoulds" you've heard have been helpful, but I suspect many others have been destructive, demeaning, and misdirecting to your life's course.

When a big decision is facing us, we often turn to others to help us decide what is the best thing for us to do. Because we may not be sure of ourselves, we want others' input. And others love to give advice and love to have you join them in their way of thinking and living if possible, even if joining them isn't truly the best thing for you.

Many will say, "You should be doing it this way." This can be a shaming message. It implies what you are doing now is wrong, and if you want to do it right, you should do it their way. You don't want to do it wrong, so you've listened to these messages from the time you were a child until now.

But how is it working, living the life others say you should live?

## So Many "You Shoulds"

When it comes to your major life choices, love, and relationships, only you can determine what is the best way for you to go. To make that decision, you've got to know what is you and what is someone else.

The following are some of the most common and most destructive "You Shoulds" that may be running in your unconscious.

### ✦ You Should Obey God or Be Condemned

In all my years of self examination, psychology, and spiritual study, I can say without hesitation that nothing I've seen has caused more psychic damage to people than this message. I remember a bedtime prayer I was taught:

> *Now I lay me down to sleep.*
> *I pray the Lord my soul to keep;*
> *But if I die before I wake,*
> *I pray the Lord my soul to take.*

What? "If I die before I wake ..." How is a six-year-old supposed to get to sleep thinking he could die that night and possibly end up in hell for some wrongdoing?

Religious messages taught to us by misguided messengers take a serious toll on our perspective of Spirit. Some of us have been so beaten down and turned off by others who use "God's Word" as a weapon to make us wrong that we no longer want to have anything to do with God or even want to hear of it. The fear and shame of being condemned by God for a mistake can be haunting to us, especially when we are children, which is often when these messages get embedded inside us.

For thousands of years, man has manipulated "the Word of God" to meet his own egoic desires and to control others. There really is no greater lever over others than someone in religious or political authority telling his subjects, "Do what God says, or you'll burn in hell" or "Do what God says, and you'll have everlasting life!" What the authorities in truth are usually saying is, "Do what I'm telling you to do because this is how I interpreted God's Word to meet my particular needs and agenda."

This is really serious business, and shaming messages have sent many of us into drugs, alcohol, and other destructive escapes trying to rid ourselves of religious guilt. Hearing for years how it's a sin to do this or do that and how God is going to punish us can really screw up our heads. Many of us have given up, thinking we can never be good enough for God.

Thinking that God wants to torture me for a mistake isn't the God I ever wanted to have. So after my life hit rock bottom, I wanted and needed a spiritual Source to help me; but I wanted another God, not the God of my childhood teachings. I wanted a Force that would love me, One that could bring me peace and not guilt me, so I went looking.

And instead of looking forever out in the world for It, I looked within myself. I figured if "God is everywhere," as my priests once said, then that Force is inside me as well. I chose to no longer listen to man's interpretation of what God is saying and instead to go straight to the Source. I cut out the middle man and began to listen to my Inner Voice that directed me. That Voice directed me to love and peace. Instead of knowing about God, I began to experience God—which came in the form of love and connection.

If your messages about God are keeping you down instead of lifting you up, it's time to look for some new messages. There is a loving voice inside you that will lift you up. Although it may be muffled, it is there. You have to clear out the old negative voices, so you can hear the loving One of your Soul.

Making this connection begins by looking for the light and the love in everyone and every situation. By moving towards loving thoughts, your mind will come closer to peace and the experience of a Loving Force will start to appear for you, within you. And It will show up in connections and feelings of love with others.

### ✦ You Should Never Disagree with Your Parents or Authority Figures

Not everything your parents and teachers said to you or taught you was right for you. And much of it wasn't right for them either, but they continued to pass these messages because it's all they knew. And it's very difficult for the ego of someone who's in an authority position to hear himself say, "I don't know." It takes a pretty secure person to say those words.

Trust in your own inner guide, and trust in your own experiences. Just because you read something, hear something, or see someone on TV who appears to be an expert doesn't mean their message is true or right or for your life. Listen to others' good counsel, but use your own discernment to decide what is best.

Be the authority of your own life. Trust yourself, and trust the Voice inside that inspires you.

### ✦ You Should Sacrifice Yourself for Those You Love

Sacrifice implies pain and suffering for another's benefit. There is rarely a time when you have to sacrifice your own well-being for those you love. If that time comes, I strongly encourage you to deeply contemplate that decision.

When you are in the realm of love, there isn't sacrifice. Giving to another is done by choice; and in giving, you feel a deeper connection to the loving Soul. It should fill you up, not deprive you. If you don't feel that, something isn't right. For example, getting up in the middle of the night to care for someone could be considered a sacrifice with physical stress, loss of sleep, and irritation as the consequences. Or it could be a loving act with energizing joy as the reward for being of service to another in need. It's a matter of where your heart and mind are in the moment.

If you are in pain as a result of giving to another, you are not in the realm of the Soul. Change your intentions! Your pain is a result of your not being aligned correctly with loving intention. Love is not hurting yourself to help another. Loving action benefits everyone involved. When you do something out of love, there is no psychic suffering or sacrifice, only more love and peace to be gained.

## ✦ You Should Never Break a Promise or a Commitment

Integrity is about keeping your word and commitments. It is an admirable quality, one that is at the foundation of all connected relationships. Integrity is also about living your truth, where your internal thoughts and feelings are aligned with your external actions.

Without integrity, peace is not possible. However, there is a time when promises and commitments must be broken with others in order to maintain integrity with your Soul. Oftentimes, we make commitments and then the circumstances change, which changes our ability maintain the agreement. Or we change our minds because we wake up and realize that what we committed to is really not a good fit.

When your outer commitments conflict with what is true and right for you inside, this is a time when those outer commitments need to be renegotiated. Only you know which commitments you must keep and which you must break or renegotiate. There is often a way to break promises and commitments with integrity that leaves everyone whole. The most appropriate time to discuss a change in a commitment is before it is broken.

There will be times when following the inner guidance of your heart will leave someone else feeling hurt or disappointed. This is when you must ask yourself, "How committed are you to living the life that your inner compass is directing you to live, and are you willing to disappoint another to be true to yourself? If you can find the strength to live your inner truth, you'll find a life full of freedom, love, and joy.

### ✦ You Should Know Better

If you consciously knew better, you obviously wouldn't have done it the way you did, so don't beat yourself up. "Fall down six times, get up seven" is an old saying meant to inspire you to shake off your mistakes and keep on going. Although the math is wrong, the message is wise: Keep getting up from your mistakes!

Life is full of errors and lessons. We can only do the best we can in the moment with what knowledge we have. For those of us that carry this message, we can freeze up when a new opportunity or challenge presents itself. We don't want to be shamed or look foolish in front of others; so instead of admitting we don't know or trying, we do nothing. We don't risk anything because we don't want to be wrong. Because we were shamed greatly for mistakes as children, we are scared to death to make any more. And this stops us from extending or experiencing love and life fully.

It is inevitable that you must risk making a mistake in order to align with the life that is meant for you. Some of us are so off-course that we have to try a few paths, some of which will be the wrong ones, before we find the right one. You have to learn to accept that you will make a mistake and that you are okay if you make one or two or ten thousand. The goal is to learn from your mistakes so they aren't wasted. And that takes however long it takes.

### ✦ You Should Get Married, Get a 'Real Job,' Make Money, Buy a Home, Have Kids, Be Happy

This life prescription may be for you, and it may not be. The societal pressure to be married along with the lack of control you have over another person, a prospective spouse, make this "should" especially haunting to singles. The message is, "If you're not married with a family and a home, you're not doing life right, you're not good enough, you are somehow missing out on a chance for love and happiness."

Being married with kids and a home has nothing to do with your lovability, worthiness, or happiness. Married life is a lifestyle choice, and because you haven't made that choice doesn't mean there is anything wrong with that or wrong with you. If you feel insecure and unworthy because you're not living the married life, this is an area for you to grow through. Marriage can't give you inner security. You have to find peace within yourself. That is between you and the Divine. And marriage isn't for everyone. Obviously. Look at the divorce statistics.

Having children isn't a requirement. Children can't bring you peace. Owning a home isn't for everyone. A house can't make you happy.

Working nine to five isn't the only way; it never was for me, but it is for some.

Be confident in yourself. Being single is no worse and no better than being married. It's just another form of being, another life-style, another choice. Only your opinion of yourself makes one choice better than the other.

You don't need what the world says you need to be very happy. The experience of connected love is what everyone really wants, and that can be had. So live your own life. Face any fears you have. It's the only way to truly live.

### ✦ You Should Be With Him/Marry Him Because You Are "in Love"

Loving another is a natural and common thing. If you are a loving person, you will be finding love for many people. But we've been taught to believe that if you really love someone passionately, you should intertwine your lives or get married. Just because you love someone doesn't mean you have to attach yourself to him or that it is even a good idea, especially in some situations.

For example, you can deeply love someone who is an active heroin addict, but it may not be the smartest, most healthy move to marry him or have him living in your home. You can deeply love a kleptomaniac, but you will want to keep your hand on your wallet. Loving someone doesn't mean you stop thinking and making smart, self-supportive, self-loving decisions.

Love is not scarce; there isn't only one person out there for you to share love with. In fact, it's quite the opposite. And you don't have to hold on to and contain someone to experience love with them. Loving someone is one thing. Being compatible to share your lives together is a whole other issue. Love doesn't require anything; it exists as it is.

### ✦ You Should Make Your Relationship Last

Some relationships last a lifetime; some last a few minutes. It's not always up to you how long you will have an active relationship with someone. And it's not up to you to determine what the purpose of that relationship will be.

You can have a very connected, love-filled encounter with someone that may only last a moment in time and then he is out of your life. You may have another relationship full of turbulence and heartache with someone that stays around for 50 years.

Don't be concerned about the duration of relationships. The quality of a relationship is not measured by how long it lasts in a particular form. The quality of a relationship is measured by the amount of love experienced inside of you.

## ✦ You Should Stay in an Unfulfilling/Unhappy Marriage for the Kids

The question to ask yourself with this "should" is, *Are you truly staying for the benefit of the kids, or are you staying because you're afraid to face your own fears?* I know as a child, I would rather have been *from* a broken home than living *in* a broken home.

You may also want to ask yourself, *Am I being a good role model for my children by staying in a dysfunctional situation?* Your children will likely mimic your relationship when they begin to have their own adult relationships. They do what they know; and if they only know how to be in an ugly, dysfunctional, love-starved relationship, that is likely their destiny.

It's a lack of loving experiences that hurts children. It's a lack of love overshadowed by fear that causes the painful wounds.

Fear and separation are contagious. If you as a parent feel fear and disconnection in your home life, the children will feel it. Children need to be surrounded by loving people in a loving environment.

If it's not possible in the current situation, find a way out and into a peaceful, loving situation. We all need to have love flourishing around us. If it can't flourish where you are, change it. Change it for yourself, and change it for your children. Do whatever you need to open the channel of love back into your heart. Free yourself to love more fully, and those around you will benefit.

### ✦ You Should Never Get Divorced

There is nothing spiritually or morally wrong with divorce. There is something spiritually and morally wrong with not loving one another. It's not the dissolution of a marriage that is so painful, but the dissolution of love between people that is so painful.

The only thing that stays the same in this life is change, so you have to become comfortable with that. And in order to be at peace and in the flow of love, you must be able to bend and flex with the changes.

You may not be able to live with someone anymore. You may not want to be romantic or sexual with your spouse. You may now disagree about how you both want to live your lives. Because of these differences or changes, it may not be possible to be happy and be together in the same way. What *was* is not now, and it's time to make the adjustments.

However, the end of the form of a marriage doesn't have to be the end of a loving relationship. You can still find love for one another and help each other grow, even if it is in separate directions. Loving someone fully sometimes means leaving him, not only for your benefit, but so he can go find what is awaiting him. Spiritual connection is not concerned with the form a relationship takes, only the content of the love.

### ✦ You Should Stay in the Relationship/Break Up

When someone tells you to leave a relationship, it might be wise to listen to them. They may be seeing something you are denying. Equally, it might be wise to not listen to them. No one knows your situation better than you do, and their advice may be way off-base.

You know inside yourself if it is time to leave for your own good and the good of everyone involved. Trust in that over everything else, listen to it, and act. If your Heart tells you to keep working and stay, do it! If your Heart tells you it's time to go, go! And don't let fear be the deciding vote.

It's usually fairly easy to determine for yourself if it's right to stay or go. A teacher once asked me, "Does being in this relationship bring you more peace than you'd have if you were not in it?" How you answer this will tell you a lot. If a relationship isn't peace-bringing, you've got to ask yourself, *Why am I staying with it?*

In my experience, in order to live peacefully, you can't have too many toxic or troublesome people in your life. If you associate with negative, complaining, or attack-minded people, you will likely become more negative, complaining, and attack-minded. If you associate with loving, happy people, you're likely to become more loving and happy. It's wise to guard your peaceful inner state of being by keeping those who would disrupt that at a distance.

### ✦ You Should Always Be Happy

We're trained to put on our happy face for the world and pretend everything is wonderful, even in times when it's everything but. Of all the various emotions we can feel, happiness is just one. Yet it's the only emotion society gives us the okay to feel.

The truth is, you can't always be happy. And it's not healthy to always try to be. Whatever you are feeling is what you are feeling; go with it. If you are sad, grieving, or hurting, that is where you are right now. If you are angry, be angry. It's okay to be with whatever emotion you are experiencing.

By trying to force yourself or pretending to be happy when you're not, you only prolong your internal suffering. And what makes it worse is the fear of not always being happy.

We have to accept that there will be times in life when we will feel many other things, and happiness won't be one of them. It's okay. It's expected. It's healthy. Although it may not be what we want to feel, uncomfortable or painful feelings are perfectly natural. Do not resist them. You can be at peace with whatever you are feeling. This is the goal—peacefulness with whatever comes.

### ✦ You Should Be Strong/Not Cry

Blocking yourself from crying and grieving is like blocking yourself from urinating. In time, it's going to cause some serious internal damage.

Crying is the body's removal system for emotional toxins that get built up over time. It has to happen, or problems will occur. Without release, your mind and emotional body get overloaded and emotional disease like depression sets in. So let it out.

Crying is a natural function, and allowing yourself to cry is a sign of true internal strength. It takes courage to let go. It takes courage to stand in the face of a myth that says, "You're weak if you cry." It takes courage to be with a feeling that is uncomfortable, but crying will refresh you. It will unclog your pathway to the Soul. Cry and you will heal. Cry and you will remove what blocks love.

### ✦ You Should Be More Successful

Success for the ego can be judged by many standards. The only success that is deeply fulfilling and that really matters to your Soul is how much love you are experiencing in your life. All other forms of success pale in comparison to the rewards that a rich loving life provides.

You don't need money, education, or good fortune to accomplish this. Kindness and a willingness to serve others will bring more inner success to you than you can imagine.

### ✦ You Should Be _____ (a Doctor, a Lawyer, a Teacher, etc.)

Our society generates a lot of pressure to be successful in "prestigious" careers. Others often project their beliefs and self-serving wants for their lives onto you. The message in my family's history was that the only true professionals were doctors and lawyers, and we have several generations of doctors as a result.

But you have a true inner calling, and it may or may not lead you in a direction that others find "desirable." Finding your life's career is far less important than finding your passion that will allow you to serve others and fill your Soul. If your passion is serving others through the work that you do, or if you can make your work a means for serving others, you will experience success. You will feel more peace, and connection to others and love will flow in your life.

### ✦ You Should Be More Like Others, So You Can Fit In and Be Accepted

We all want to fit in, to be loved and appreciated by others but not at the risk of sacrificing our values. When you surrender what is important to you to get approval from another, you won't have your own approval. This is a much harder conflict to live with.

For years, I wore a suit and tie to work because I thought I should. I thought I was supposed to look professional, so others would do business with me and accept me. I was in a business where everyone wore suits. But I was really uncomfortable in a suit. It was constrictive, hot, and not compatible with my personality.

One day, I gave all my suits away and pledged to never wear another unless I wanted to. It's been 15 years, and I still haven't worn one. My life is better, not only because I'm not wearing a suit but because I'm living a life that is more me.

Another example was drinking alcohol. I used to drink, and nearly everyone around me drank. I really didn't like the scene, the way it made me feel or act, so I quit. For a while, it was hard because people were always offering me drinks and feeling rejected when I didn't want to drink with them. It wasn't personal, but many made it so, and I lost some friends.

Since I wasn't out drinking, I had to find something else to do. This is where I started to find the things I really enjoyed doing.

Thoreau said, "If a man doesn't keep pace with his companions, perhaps it is because he hears a different drummer. Let him step to the music which he hears, however measured or far away." The closer you can come to living the way you really want to, the happier you will be. Not living your own life is like wearing someone else's shoes—you might get them on your feet, but it's not a comfortable way to walk through town. So do a lot more of what you want to do and a lot less of what you don't.

### ✦ You Should Be Better Than You Are

This is the master key of all these destructive messages. If you're not tormenting yourself with one of the previous "shoulds," you will likely use this as a catch-all. This message has many variations such as, "You should be thinner, prettier, smarter, taller, richer, younger," and so on.

The basic message and the way we typically interpret this is, "You're not good enough as you are now!" This is a devastating message to our sense of self. This voice from our ego is what keeps us from really loving. It's impossible to love ourselves when we are hearing things in our minds like, *You're not good enough for him, for your kids, for this relationship, for this life, for Heaven.* If you don't feel lovable, you can't see others as lovable.

Stop listening to that destructive, untrue voice. Begin telling yourself you are good enough. You may not hear it or want to believe it at first, but keep telling yourself this. It's true. You are good enough; and when you start to believe it, love will flow.

### HEARING "YOU SHOULD" AND REMOVING IT

The next time you're faced with a decision or you are feeling disturbed by one you've already made, ask yourself, *Am I hearing "You should" in the back ground of my thoughts?* Listen to the old tape that plays "You should," and when you hear it, eject it!

Stop taking the old directions from others that you hear inside your head without considering your own. Be a rebel in the face of those messages that try to control you and keep your life conformed to someone else's wishes. Be your own person and follow the voice of your Soul.

You know from your own experience that not listening to your Inner Voice almost always ends painfully. Living your own life and following your truth can at times be a lonely path because most will take the sheep trail, doing what others say they "should."

It takes a great deal of courage to be who you really are. But how else can you live with yourself?

When it comes to giving advice to others, it's best to avoid telling them "You should." You don't really know what someone else should do and, as we have discussed here, it has a shaming tone to it. You don't want to make someone you're trying to support feel they are in the wrong.

You want to be helpful, kind and encouraging. Instead, it's more loving to say, "I'd encourage you to …" or "Have you considered doing …"

It allows someone to make their own decision from within themselves and is supportive of whatever they ultimately decide. Others are going to remember and appreciate the way you were with them more than they will appreciate what you told them. So help them find the message their Soul is telling them, and everyone will benefit.

# CHAPTER 10

# Clean Up Your Side of the Street

*What you do speaks so loudly
that I cannot hear what you say.*

—Ralph Waldo Emerson

*W*ith every person you meet and every relationship you have, there is the potential for a Soul-connection, but you may have psychological or behavioral blocks that prevent you from stepping into the experience.

Pop psychologists like to call these blocks "baggage." Baggage is the wounds, fears, defenses, and illusions you carry from your past into your present relationships. If you have baggage, you will have trouble feeling at ease within yourself at times. If you can't feel at ease within yourself, your relationships won't be easy.

Someone's inner baggage is what usually derails a relationship from reaching its potential; sometimes it's your baggage, sometimes it's theirs. It's much easier to see their baggage than it is to see your own. Generally speaking, we are all very good at analyzing and pointing out the misgivings in others but not very good in seeing those things in ourselves.

Your ego aspect always prefers to blame someone else for messing things up in your relationships. However, since you don't have any real control over others, the best chance you have at immediately improving your relationships is by improving yourself.

This begins by awakening to your own thoughts and behavior. The work is here, with you; and if you can make some alterations to the way you relate, you will see some immediate results. You don't have to change the world to find peace; you just have to change the way you experience and relate to the world.

You don't have to grow into being Soul-connected because you already are. It's built into you. You just may not be able to find that place because of all the inner baggage you've accumulated and carry around with you. Spiritual growth in this context is not an accumulation of all-new information but a purging of the old information that is blocking you. It's about cleaning up the inner debris that clutters your heart.

There are some major things you can start practicing right now that will go a long way toward clearing a space for love and connection to happen.

## What Is Yours and What Is Theirs

It's been said that a relationship with another is a two-way street. If this is true, then you've got to know which side is yours to drive on.

What often happens in close relationships—whether between good friends, children, family, or romantic partners—is that the people involved drive all over each other's sides of the street. This is called enmeshment.

When you are enmeshed with someone, you aren't clear where you, your feelings, and your responsibilities end and theirs begin. In the quest for union and closeness, the boundary that separates the two of you gets blurred to a point where you each lose your autonomy.

When this happens, the relationship usually takes an ugly turn for the worse, with each one blaming the other for their unhappiness. This common situation is one that played out before me with some friends I know, exactly during the time I was writing this chapter.

Tom and Cindy have lived together for five years.

Over the last few years, Cindy has become more involved in health and fitness lifestyle. She has quit drinking, watches what she eats, exercises, and does yoga nearly every day. Tom drinks a lot of beer, eats junk, and thinks riding in a golf cart for 18 holes is exercise; he tells Cindy he isn't that interested in the whole fitness thing. No matter, she still tries to motivate him; but he doesn't do much, so she tries even harder.

Cindy now spends much of her time angry with Tom and frequently fighting with him over this. She feels betrayed and blames him for it. She feels rejected because he won't take care of himself and do what she thinks is best. She says that his poor health habits are going to destroy their relationship. She believes that it's her responsibility to get him healthy. Every time she sees him eating something fried or pulling out another beer, she gets very upset and communications spiral down from there, usually into an upsetting fight.

This is a common and classic situation of enmeshment, where one person gets into another's business. Because they are in a close relationship, Cindy thinks Tom's business is her business as well. Fact is, Tom's health habits are truly his business, and Cindy's are hers. Cindy wants him to be healthy, she wants the relationship to be healthy, she cares for him, and she feels fear inside; but these are her feelings, wants, and beliefs. Not his. This problem lies on her side of the street.

If he wants to be healthy, that is up to him. Aside from Cindy's fear-based emotional attachment, Tom's behavior is only affecting Tom. He is not responsible for her being upset; only she is. But she certainly doesn't have to be. She can love and accept him as is, or she can choose to be upset. She can decide what she wants to do for herself but what he does for himself is his business.

It's important for you to check yourself frequently and see if you are getting into someone else's business. Are your fears and concerns driving you across the street to their side? It's common to try to work, manipulate, and persuade others to your point of view, but you're often out of your lane.

If you are doing it so you feel more comfortable or to pacify your own fear, you need to get back on your side of the street and deal with that fear within yourself. Trying to get someone to be different doesn't come across as loving. If you're not sure if you do this or you're not aware, the next time you begin to tell someone what to do, ask yourself:

- Am I making the business of their life, their body, their emotions mine?

- Am I telling them what to do to make myself more comfortable?

- Am I trying to fix their problem?

- Would I want them showing up in my life like I'm about to show up in theirs?

If you are out of your lane, you can always steer over and get back to your side. Watching yourself and correcting yourself in this area will remove a significant amount of conflict from your relationships. And this is something you have a great deal of control over.

However, sometimes other people will drive across the street and up onto your sidewalk. Others will get into your business, making you responsible for their feelings and their situation. What do you do then?

Just the other night, I was on the phone with Brenda, a woman I've been dating exclusively for many months. Another call that I was expecting came in on my office line. I answered it. "Hi, Stacey! I'm on the other line. Can I call you back in ten minutes?" She agreed, and I hung up and went back to my call with Brenda.

Brenda was now fuming, "Who's Stacy? Is this some woman

you're dating I don't know about? It's late. Why is she calling you so late? What's up with that? I can't trust you anymore!" She became more upset the more she vented but really had no information other than what she was making up in her head about this. In her mind, I became the bad guy who was lying and cheating, and it was all my fault she felt the way she did.

When I finally got a chance to talk, I explained as much as I could without breaking confidentiality. Truth was, Stacy was a counseling client I had asked to call me at a specific time. She was going on her first date, sober, which was a very big and potentially risky situation for her.

Brenda didn't like my explanation, didn't trust it, but I couldn't do a lot more about it. It was the truth, and there was no more to it.

This was something Brenda was going to have to work out for herself. It was her side of the street stuff. I couldn't fix it, and I knew it. But part of me, my ego, started to rise up, and I wanted to defend myself aggressively. Fortunately, I allowed myself to breathe for a moment and chose to let her keep her issue, her issue.

As we discussed this again a few days later, I found out more. Brenda's ex-husband had lied and cheated on her, and this situation was triggering that old baggage. It really wasn't about me at all; it wasn't anything that I had done or not done. My situation was just a trigger for her.

When you find yourself in the situation of being blamed for something or someone else's feelings that you don't have control over, you want to recognize that this is their baggage, and it's not your side of the street stuff.

You can be compassionate, reassuring and comforting, but do not allow their inner drama to become your inner drama. Stay at peace within yourself. Sometimes you can be of help with them getting through it, and sometimes you can't. You can be solid in yourself, autonomous, and still loving.

The Sufi poet Kahlil Gibran said, "Let there be spaces in your togetherness, and let the winds of the heavens dance between you. Love one another, but make not a bond of love: let it rather be a moving sea between the shores of your souls." Loving someone, being very open and closely intimate, doesn't mean you have to lose who you are.

You don't have to be emotionally affected or react to their drama. You can lovingly let it be their drama. Know that you are separate people, with separate bodies, brains, feelings, reactions, perceptions, beliefs.

Achieving Oneness in Spirit doesn't mean your humanness is joined. It means that at the deepest level, you understand the human experience; it means you have an unconditional, Soul-centered love for one another that connects you regardless of human differences. And this connection can grow stronger when there is a mutual respect and understanding for each other's own worldly, human individuality.

## LET GO AND LET IT BE

There is a message that is becoming hugely popular among the self-growth community: You are 100% in charge of your life, you can manifest anything you want just by thinking positively about it and really wanting it to happen.

Many books, CDs, and movies have been made that tell you how you can create money, cars, houses, lovers, a husband, a wife, or anything else you want just by focusing your mind on it. They tell you that you control your life, your destiny, your relationships and that you can have everything you desire just by wanting it bad enough. It's been called the Law of Attraction. And this message is very inspirational. And they are right. Up to a point.

You do have a significant part in creating your life and your relationships. You can effect situations, you can choose directions,

and most importantly you can choose how you experience the outcome of many situations; but you are not ultimately in control of
those outcomes no matter how much you think you are. When it
comes to controlling the world, the Universe, and those around
you, at times you're really not much more powerful than a flea who
is trying to control the dog he sits on. And when situations and
relationships don't go your way, the Universe is letting you know
who is ultimately in control.

So why do we try to control other people and situations? Because
we are afraid if we let go and allow things to be, the situation will
turn out badly for us. The problem with this way of thinking is it's
shortsighted and lacks faith. Our fear and feelings of need in the
moment don't allow us to see the big picture clearly.

If you've ever had an experience that you thought was bad at
the time, like a person breaking up with you or losing a job, and
upon looking back you saw how it was a really huge blessing, then
you know what I'm talking about. By trying to over-control a situation, you may be blocking the Universe from giving you what you
really need and want but just aren't aware of yet. What you think
you want may not be what is best for you.

When you are afraid of loss or change, you may try to over-
control others or those things around you. The more fear, the more
control you will try to exert. And the more you try to control someone or a situation, the more distress you're going to feel, especially
as you realize that you aren't truly in control. Trying to control
those people and situations around you is like, as they say in Texas,
"trying to herd cats." It doesn't work because it's against the natural
order. The harder you chase cats, the more they scatter; the harder
you try to control the world around you, the more chaotic it seems
to become.

In our previous example, Cindy is trying to control Tom because she is afraid of something. In her case, it wasn't so much his

health that was the issue (that was the excuse), but rather the loss of their relationship was the real underlying issue. She had lost her physical attraction for him and thought by making him get in shape and changing him that could save her. She was ultimately afraid of being alone and changing her own life; she tried to make her outer world change, so she wouldn't have to change what she was afraid of changing. The more he resisted, the closer she came to what she feared. This made her even more desperate inside and more controlling.

As soon as you try to avoid anything, you are going to have to control everything. And this can consume your life and become exhausting.

Cindy couldn't avoid the truth any longer, eventually she faced her fear, accepted that she wasn't going to change Tom and shouldn't try. She surrendered. And then she realized that the best thing for his and her peace was to split. She let go of control, allowed him to be who he is, where he is; and she is much happier living by herself.

She's now dating someone much more compatible to her life-style. Tom progressed in his alcohol use until legal circumstances and a family intervention brought him into treatment and recovery. They are now much better friends as a result of all the changes.

The experience Cindy was ultimately wanting was right around a blind corner; she was just afraid to let go and trust. The Soul-connected, enlightened mindset is not one of "I'm in control; I create what happens" but one of "I do what I can; I co-create in harmony with the Universe and trust It to ultimately control what happens."

A spiritual teacher once said to me, "Mike, your life is really none of your business," which confused me at first.

When I finally figured it out, it made perfect sense and brought me to a place of peace. If I was in control of my life, you wouldn't be reading this book right now because when I was young, I wanted to play pro football. Being five-foot-eight, 150 pounds, not very fast, and not all that good didn't make me a viable candidate for my chosen life. And if I was in control of my relationships, I would have married my high-school sweetheart over 20 years ago. But she had other plans. And so did I apparently.

So getting the things you want isn't the path to peace. It's getting on board with what the Universe wants for you that is the path to peace. It's about living in alignment with Universe's prescription for your life.

Letting go and allowing everything to be as it is, is about remaining flexible and welcoming whatever comes in whatever way it shows up. It's about allowing others to be who they are and loving them as they are now. It means that nothing or no one has to change in order for you to be okay or to be loving. This doesn't mean being apathetic or lazy. It means being flexible and open to different directions. So start letting go, relax your mind and your body, and let things be in the care of an Order much more powerful than you. You will find that if you do, you will get what your Soul really wants for you.

## MAKING AMENDS

It's difficult to create connected, loving relationships in the present when you have wounded relationship energy still lingering from the past. A relationship situation you've had that resulted in disconnection or hurt for the other person can cause you to carry destructive energy inside you, another form of baggage. A lot of times this shows up as guilt or shame; and you may not even be fully conscious of how it is affecting you.

The way this works is simple. You can't harm another without harming yourself in some way. You can't have ill thoughts about someone without it disturbing you on the inside. And anytime you treat another unlovingly, there is a place inside you that will suffer a wound. Our natural state is to feel connected; disconnection in any form can create hurt inside you. At this level, we are all the same. The only difference is that some are aware of how this affects them and some are not.

If you're not sure about the validity of this idea, for a few moments just try thinking about doing harm to one of your pets or loved ones and notice how you feel inside. The thought alone is enough to create some very uncomfortable energy inside you. It's upsetting. And if you actually carried it out, it would be even more upsetting. So any place in your life where you've done wrong by another and not cleared it up, there is a wound inside you. And possibly one inside them as well.

The good news is you can change all that. You can correct it.

I went for years totally unconscious of my behavior in relationships. On the advice of a counselor, I scanned my relationship history, looking for how I was hurtful and unloving towards others throughout my past. I found multiple instances, especially with my family and my romantic relationships. I realized that I was pretty coldhearted, judgmental, disrespectful, and distant to people at times. Many people who showed me love I snubbed in return.

At the time I was spreading this toxicity, I had no awareness of how my actions were affecting others or myself. I was going through life self-consumed, fearful, and unconscious. But once I awoke to this truth, I wanted to do something to help mend those wounded relationships. Or at least take responsibility for my part and try to find some inner peace.

You can't change what happened in the past, but you can change the way you experience the past by healing those lingering wounds in the present.

The ego always wants to blame someone else for the problem. In order to free yourself, you have to take complete responsibility for your actions. You have to look inside yourself and identify where you missed the mark. You may not be 100% responsible for the mess, but you are 100% responsible for your part of the mess, and you can do something about your part. And that is enough because that is all you can do.

How do you know whom you need to make amends to? If there is anyone you feel uneasy around, or uncomfortable running into face to face, or someone you want to avoid because of a past incident, then that is certainly a relationship that begs to be restored to wholeness. If when you scan your relationship history, you find times you've been unloving or hurtful towards another, this is a relationship that wants to be healed.

And remember this, healing a relationship in part is healing the way *you* experience the relationship. They may or may not want to clean up the relationship, but that is not your concern. You can't change them or their perception. You can't clean their side of the street for them, but you can clean up yours.

Making amends to another can take many forms. In some of my cases with ex-girlfriends, I chose to call them on the phone; others that I knew were married I chose to write letters to because I felt it inappropriate to be invasive; others I spoke with face to face. How you do it is not as important as doing it. Here are some guidelines you can follow that will keep it clean.

1. Take the mindset of full responsibility for your part in what happened.

2. Decide the best, most suitable way to contact the person or people involved.

3. State to them the data, the facts of what happened, the way you experienced it.

4. Fully own your mistake by telling them what you were thinking and feeling at the time.

5. Communicate what you are thinking and feeling about the situation now.

6. Speak to what you want for the relationship, for you and for them.

7. Release your attachment to any particular outcome or response by them and accept what is now.

In making amends I found it best to fully own my mistakes and behavior. I made it about me and made sure I wasn't pointing the finger at anyone else. I've also found that saying "I'm sorry" alone doesn't cut it. When you really want to be real with someone, you want to tell them your deeper truth, even if you're embarrassed about it.

Owning your mistakes and unloving behavior serves two main purposes: It helps to heal you, and it creates an opportunity to heal another. An amends may look something like this part of a letter I wrote to an ex-girlfriend:

*It's been years since we last talked, and I believe I owe you an explanation. When we got in that last fight, I walked away and never communicated with you again. I didn't take your calls and avoided seeing you in public. I left things incomplete, left many things unspoken, and that was an insensitive way to handle it. I was wrong to do that. I wouldn't want anyone to abandon me in that way, and I wish I had done it differently. Truth was, I was scared. I had strong, loving feelings for you, and I was afraid of being hurt, so I foolishly ran. At that time of my life, I was really a mess; I didn't have a clue how to love someone or treat someone lovingly. I want you to know that it wasn't about you; it wasn't something you did. I was in a bad place inside my-*

*self for a long time and didn't even know it. Now I do, now
I see what a reckless, hurtful mistake it was. I handled that
situation very poorly, and I feel sad and ashamed for it.*

*I understand you are married now, and I'm not wanting
to stir anything up or cause any problems. I just wanted to
let you know what was really true for me. I still carry very
fond memories of you and feel love in my heart for you. If at
some point you feel you have something you want to say to
me, I'm open and will welcome whatever it is. I wish you the
best. Sincerely, Mike*

Even though many of the contacts were a bit scary for me to
make at first, every contact was ultimately empowering. After each
call, letter, and meeting, more energy returned to my body. I felt
peace coming into me. Even with those who never responded to
my letters I now feel at peace, knowing that I have owned my part.
Even those who called back with some harsh words for me ultimately helped with our mutual healing.

Taking care of this part of my past brought me back into integrity with myself. I felt much more okay with me, and this was life
changing. It will likely be for you as well. It's never too late to bring
love to any situation.

## CLEAR UNFINISHED BUSINESS

Another thing that can keep you blocked is having unfinished
business with yourself and others. Have you ever committed to do
something, and you haven't done it yet? No matter what commitment you've made, those commitments you haven't brought to a
place of completion can deplete your energy and block you from
feeling connected. And in time, if you have several, they can eventually add up to a huge, debilitating load to carry around. Even
small things, like telling a friend you will call them sometime to

meet for lunch and not following through, can effect you; they all add up. And some of the heaviest are the promises you quietly make to yourself that haven't been completed.

Writing this book is an example of a promise I made to myself. For a very long time, I kept putting it on the back burner and only dabbling with it, not making any real, substantial progress. I would feel my energy drain every time I thought about how I wasn't moving forward.

Over a few years of doing research and interviews, I told a lot of people I was writing a book, so I felt committed to them as well. At one point, I thought about giving it up, that it was just too much work, but my Soul wouldn't let me. It was something I wanted to do and had to do if I was going to be at peace with myself.

Many things can show up like this. Any time you have a calling from inside yourself, it has to be answered and followed through with. Otherwise you won't feel connected. If you feel called to speak out about something, you must do it. If you feel compelled to tell someone how you feel, do it. You will feel invigorated.

Don't leave commitments hanging out there. If you've made commitments to others and not yet followed through, you must address them, even if it means contacting them to tell them you're not going to be able to follow through.

Don't ignore your Inner Voice. If you do, the incompleteness will leave you feeling encumbered, and you won't be free to connect.

And don't let the fear of what others think keep you from taking care of what you must to do to live in alignment with your Soul's direction for you. Dr. Seuss said, "Be who you are and say what you feel because those who mind don't matter and those who matter don't mind."

## OWN YOUR PROJECTIONS

Much of what we do and think about in life is unconscious. You probably are not aware you are breathing, at least not until I brought it up and pointed it out to you now. There are a lot of things you do and think about that are just beyond your awareness.

One of the most important to your relationships and most potentially dangerous to your peace is that of projection. Unconscious breathing isn't a problem for your relationships, but unconscious projecting is. Projecting onto others is responsible for everything from hurt feelings between friends to major world wars.

Projection is a tricky manipulation your ego plays on you. It's difficult to grasp and understand it, which is the ego's intent. The ego would much rather have you not understand the concept and just blame others. The concept is also a bit difficult to explain but easy to experience, so we'll start with that.

Let's say you write me inviting me to dinner. I do not respond. As you process this lack of response, your mind starts to play games with the hidden meanings behind my lack of response. Depending on your ego's state, you might react inside with, *Is he is mad at me? He doesn't like me. Did I do something wrong? No, he's just being a jerk.* Or something like that.

Your ego wants to know more and make someone wrong. It doesn't accept no response; it wants to give some negative meaning to it. But you don't have any information, so the ego starts to make things up about what I meant by not responding. The thoughts that your mind begins to make up and put back on me is the projection.

A projection is a reflection of one's own inner experience transposed onto another. Just as a movie projector takes an image that is internalized within the machine and then projected across the room onto a screen where it can be viewed, this is also how relationship projections work.

You take your own, unconscious internal state and project it out across the room onto another person. So if you are unconsciously angry and aggressive one day, you may experience others around you as angry and aggressive. You may even point your finger and blame someone for showing up angry and starting a fight when in actuality it was you that showed up angry and started the fight. And this kind of thing happens all the time in the world.

A projection is placing or perceiving a trait in another person that you have not fully recognized within yourself. Seeing a behavior or trait in another that triggers you emotionally in some upsetting way is a projection. And there are two common ways of projecting we're going to look at, both of which can cause damage to your inner peace and your relationships.

### ✦ Negative Projections

A negative projection is your perception of another with an energetic emotional charge attached to that you have determined to be a "bad" quality. What is one of your pet peeves about others? What is a personality trait that some people have that really annoys or upsets you? These are most likely going to be projections. Here's what one looks like.

My friend Nick gets very upset when people are late. The other day, we were going to dinner, and our friends meeting us were 30 minutes late. From the time of our reservation to the time they showed, he was consumed with it, "I can't believe they are so late. They never respect others' time. I'm never late when they want me somewhere on time; I'm always respectful of others' time." He went on and on about it until they arrived when he immediately blasted them for being late and so disrespectful.

While all this was going on, I'm quietly thinking, *Nick may always be on time for meetings, but he borrowed my fishing rod and said he would bring it back the next day. That was two months ago, and he still has it.*

This is how we project onto others. Nick may not be late for meetings, but he shows up late in other areas of his life and is not aware of it. And if you ask him about it or point it out, he gets very defensive. He sees how others are like that but refuses to see it in himself. Aside from it making him look hypocritical to others, it takes him away from his peace, compassion, and understanding. When he doesn't recognize himself in others, he may feel momentarily superior, which the ego likes, but he feels alone and separated from them, which the Soul doesn't like.

So before you get upset and blast someone for their behavior, take a good look at yourself and ask, *How am I like that in my life? Where do I show up like this?*

You may have to look hard and in some unrelated areas; but you can be sure that if you are upset about another's character trait, there is that trait lurking somewhere unnoticed within you. There is a saying, "When you're pointing a finger at another, there are three pointing back at you!"

The way to bring peace to your relationships is by recognizing those traits within yourself and owning them. Instead of mounting your high horse of superiority over others, which separates you, stay on eye level and be someone who can see oneself in others.

By taking ownership of your projection, you can oftentimes disarm the negative emotional charge, setting yourself and others free.

On the following page is a list of a few examples of negative projections and what ownership of those projections can look like.

It takes a lot of humility and courage to set pride aside and admit when you are negatively projecting. It can be a very uncomfortable experience to tell someone else that what you thought you disliked about him or her is really something inside of you that you didn't want to acknowledge.

However, it is from this place that self-empowerment and connection is born. Once you can own these parts of yourself, you are that much closer to sharing unconditional love with yourself and others.

| PROJECTION | OWNERSHIP |
|---|---|
| Your intolerance is pissing me off! | If I were more tolerant, I'd be at peace instead. |
| You are selfish and inconsiderate! | If I were less selfish, I would support your wants. |
| You are emotionally unavailable! | I am emotionally unavailable at times, too. |
| You don't communicate your feelings! | Instead of blaming, I could speak what I feel. |
| I hate those war-mongers. | My hateful attitude is a form of war-mongering. |

## ✦ Positive Projections

A positive projection is your perception of another with an energetic emotional charge attached that you have determined to be a "good" quality. If you feel envious, jealous, or particularly impressed by someone and wish you were more like them, then you are projecting. In this case, you see and admire a quality in another, but you do not see that quality within yourself.

A positive projection on another can be as disconnecting as a negative projection. By making someone else bigger, better, or more important than you are, you create disconnection in the reverse. Being "star-struck" with a celebrity is an example of a positive projection. If you put a celebrity on a pedestal of greatness and see him or her as being better in some way or more worthy than yourself, you become separate. You give away your power. And you can do this with anyone; it doesn't have to be a celebrity.

Positive projections are very commonplace in the beginning of romantic relationships. Seeing qualities in another that you don't recognize within yourself makes the other person that much more attractive and desirable. You want those qualities! You need those qualities! At least, that's what your ego thinks. So you pursue a relationship with that person to be near or obtain those qualities. When you see another as having more than you, you give them power over you. This brings you to a place of fear and separation: "You are superior, and I am inferior." This is a place of no love.

The truth is, you have those qualities you see in another; but maybe you haven't brought them fully to the light, and it's time now. You have what you need to be happy and at peace, you just aren't seeing it. As far as the Universe is concerned, we are all equal. Spiritually speaking, no one has an advantage over anyone else. Love, peace, and connection are there for everyone.

If you see others as great but don't see yourself as great also, you are shortchanging yourself. You are not looking inside far enough because it is not possible for you to witness a quality in another without having it to a degree within yourself. For example, if you see someone as very intelligent, you must be intelligent yourself, or you would not be smart enough to recognize it in them.

On the following page is a list of examples of positive projections and what it looks like to own those projections within yourself.

With projections as with many other things, it's much easier to see this in other people. You will witness others projecting, just as I did with Nick, and many times they will be projecting onto you. This is how fights start and how wars start. Somebody may come at you blaming you, telling you that you are this way or that, saying, "You are selfish. You are inconsiderate. You are dishonest," when in actuality he is the one who is being the way he is accusing you of being.

| Projection | Ownership |
|---|---|
| She is loving, kind and beautiful! | I express love and kindness. I'm beautiful. |
| He is so funny and witty. | I get his jokes; I have funny and witty in me. |
| He is so courageous! | I face my fears; I'm courageous. |
| I see her as powerful! | I see that power inside of me. |
| You live with great integrity! | I live with great integrity by speaking my truth. |

When someone is projecting onto you, it's a difficult place for you to be because they are in their ego mindset and not open to discussion, only argument. When someone is projecting onto you, this is a test for you, a test of your ability to stay centered in yourself and in the knowing of who you are.

You can't let it get to you, you can't take it personally, or you will be moving back into your ego mind. You must allow yourself to relax, knowing that you are on your side of the street, and your side is clean. You don't have to defend, fight, or protect yourself. You can just observe, let the words fizzle out on their own, and be in a place of Soul-connected loving.

## CHAPTER 11

# Stop Judging and Start Forgiving

*Hatreds never cease in the world*
*by hating, but by loving.*

—Buddha

The act of judging launches you through the door to unhappiness, and the nature of it keeps you from being aware you're doing it. If there was only one thing I could have you take away from this book that would be the most valuable, it would be a newfound awareness of your judgment and the desire to surrender it.

So what is judgment?

Can you think back to a time where you were feeling really peaceful, happy, or excited about something or someone in your life? Then, seemingly out of nowhere, something happened that burst your bubble. The good mood you were enjoying rushed away, and an inner hostility slipped in to take its place.

The shift from peace to discontent can happen lightening fast, just as fast as it takes your mind to shift from one thought to another. Because that is exactly what's happening. One moment you're at peace, and the next you're upset. One moment you are feeling connected to something nice, and the next you're feeling separated. One moment your mind is accepting and enjoying things as they are, and the next your mind has decided, *This is un-acceptable.* It is at this very point, at this change of thoughts, where judgment has entered the process.

Any thought that takes you away from a loving thought is a judgment. Any thought that takes you out of alignment with what is, is a judgment. A judgmental thought is the opposite of a kind thought. The more you judge, the more unhappy, ill, and depressed you'll become. It has been my observation and experience that depression, addiction, anger, anxiety, and many other emotionally related issues are rooted in judgment. The more we judge, the more we suffer.

I know this first-hand because I grew up in a judgmental home. My parents grew up in judgmental homes. This way of relating was common in my family and is common in many families, but some can be much more toxic than others. If you've been one who was exposed to more criticism than affirmation, you likely have a propensity to see the world through a judgmental-critical lens. It is something you can inherit. I did.

As humans, our ego side of us likes to be in charge because we're afraid to not be in control. We want to make the decisions. We want to determine what is worthy and what is not. We want to be the judge of events and people. We like to think we know what is good or bad, right or wrong, lovable or unlovable. Behaving like we're in a position to decide the value of someone or something puts us in a place of power, however imagined and false.

The reality is we are not in charge. We are not the ultimate authority. We didn't create the world around us, so it's not up to us to judge it. And yet we do, which eventually gets us into inner trouble.

There are two main areas of judgment we're going to look at that can disrupt your loving relationship experiences and your inner peace.

## JUDGING ANOTHER

A judgment of someone is the ego mind's method of attack. Not a physical attack, like hitting someone, but a thought attack on someone's being. It's a form of violence because it violates the peace, usually your own peace; you can't think ill of someone and not have it stir you on some level. Martin Luther King, Jr., said, "Nonviolence means avoiding not only external physical violence but also internal violence of spirit. You not only refuse to shoot a man, but you refuse to hate him."

Most of your judgmental thoughts are things you would never say out loud directly to another person because you don't want to be that rude or you don't want to create a conflict. However, that doesn't matter because the conflict is already created within you. It's imagined. It is in your mind, yet it still affects you greatly; it even affects your body. Your thoughts about the person are upsetting your peace. This is an attack on you.

This concept is easily tested. Think about someone you believe has treated you poorly, someone you really don't like, and get involved in this thought. Relive what they said or did and feel what comes up for you. Before you know it, you will be worked up and your peace will be gone. That person doesn't even have to be in the room, and you will be experiencing upset. Even in their absence, you can become upset with them.

That one thought alone separates you from your Soul and peace. One simple ill thought about another is all it takes to ruin your mood. Buddha said, "Holding on to resentment is like grasping a hot coal while waiting to throw it at someone; you are the one who gets burned."

Judgment is the ego's ultimate weapon against experiencing love and connection with someone. It's the one thing that can instantly change your experience and move you to upset, fear, and the feeling of being separated from your Soul and the Soul of another.

Anytime your mind finds a character flaw in another thus making him unacceptably different, you are judging. Anytime you hold a grudge, you are judging. Anytime you feel an uneasy dislike for someone, you are judging. When you're judging, you're not loving; and when you're not loving, you will feel discomfort inside. Your ego mind is always looking for a way to kill a loving or peaceful experience with someone, and this is the number one way it does that.

What judgment says inside you is, *I can't accept you or love you because you are* _____ (Fill in the blank with something you think is unacceptable or intolerable about someone). Some of the most common excuses the ego uses to avoid unity with others are found in our associations with the following words: different, weird, ugly, fat, skinny, old, smart, stupid, rich, poor, conservative, liberal, gay, straight, white, black, communist, socialist, capitalist, my God, your God, no god, my way, your way. These are only a small fraction of the reasons the ego can use to justify disliking, hating, or, even at times for many in the world, killing others if the hateful thoughts are acted upon.

It doesn't matter what the reason may be or how right you think you are. If you are judging someone and feeling that tingle of edginess inside, you're hurting yourself and the relationship. Judgment separates you from the Divine Connection, so no matter how "bad" the person is in your opinion, your judgment of him is going to ultimately hurt you.

When you judge another, you are creating a spiritual disconnection; you are in essence taking over the role of the Divine Creator. In simple words, you're playing God. When you judge another, you are essentially deciding if that person is lovable, and that is not your decision to make.

Jesus taught love and to love your enemies. However, he didn't teach that you had to hang out with them. You may not want to hang around some people, which is fine, but it's not your place to determine their worthiness. It's not a healthy decision for you to stop your Soul from loving even when you believe the person is wrong and even when you don't like him. It is not up to any of us to decide that someone isn't worthy of our love. Soulful love that accepts others unconditionally can always be found if you look deep enough.

If you want to be at peace, you must go with the flow of what the Universe has created in the moment. You can't resist it and expect to be content and feel love. Judgment is your resistance to the experience of love and acceptance of what is. If you want out of any upsetting relationship experience, you must stop judging. It's really so simple, yet it can be so hard to let go of.

You don't have to wait on others to change. You don't have to wait on anything to be different. You can find love and peace by changing your judgmental thoughts to loving thoughts. Your mind can't hold a loving thought and a hateful thought at the same time. So, you can find peace right now by thinking about what is lovable about someone.

The other big problem with judging others is you cannot judge someone else without judging yourself. You cannot hate another unless you are experiencing self-hatred on some level. What is within you is what you put out into the world.

For example, if you judge somebody based on the way they look, perhaps you think they're inferior because they are heavier than you, then you will be judging yourself as inferior to someone who is thinner than you. If you judge someone because they have less money than you, then you are judging yourself against those who have more money than you do. It doesn't matter what method of judgment you use against someone, eventually that judgment you place on another will come back to you judging yourself, if you aren't already.

The ego doesn't care who is judged, just as long as someone is and a disconnection is created. The ego doesn't have to make any sense in its judgments either. All it is concerned with is making someone guilty and unlovable. That is it.

One of the most common situations where I see a lot of judgment happening is around religious or political discussions. People get really upset and hateful. Could you be one of them? When someone has a view that doesn't agree with yours, instead of listening and seeking to understand and accept their point of view, do you try to prove them wrong, attack them, belittle them, or overpower them to win your point? Or does someone in your life try to do that to you? Deep down, it's often not the point or position anyone is fighting to win; it is the lost connection that wants to be restored.

When you are operating from your ego mind, you don't tolerate differences. Fear comes up and the fight or flight instincts come out, which often leads to exactly what you don't want—more separation. So what if someone likes Republican over Democrat, Hinduism over Christianity? The problem here is that when you align your identity and who you are with a group, anyone who thinks differently than your group is perceived as wrong and unlovable.

If you want to get past this, you have to overcome your ego's desire to judge and separate. You have to stop comparing who is better or worse. You do not have to surrender your beliefs or convictions, just your judgment, your irritation, and whatever thought is separating you. You can still be effective in life, but you'll be doing it with inner peacefulness instead of inner turmoil. Rumi said, "If you are irritated by every rub, how can you be polished?" It is when you feel the rub that you need to practice non-judgment and extend more loving.

## Judging Situations and Events

The other way you can judge that takes you out of your Soul is by deciding which situations are good or bad, right or wrong. How you relate to situations can determine your level of peace just as much as how you relate to people. The following version of an ancient Taoist story illustrates this lesson well.

*A farmer and his young son lived together in a valley with only a few neighbors around. One night, a violent thunderstorm passed through the valley and frightened their only horse. It broke through his corral and ran far away up into the rugged, heavily forested high hills.*

*The next morning one of their neighbors, an old man, came riding down the road in his buggy and stopped to visit with the farmer and his son. The old man noticed that their horse was gone and the corral was broken. He said to the farmer in a worried voice, "This is terrible. You won't be able to plow your fields. You'll have no food. How will you survive without your horse? This is a horrible curse."*

*As the old man rode away, very upset and in deep despair, the farmer said quietly, "Maybe so."*

*The next morning the farmer awoke to see his plow horse and fourteen wild horses standing in his corral.*

*The old man rode by later, saw the horses, and said, "You got your plow horse back, and he brought all these others. You are rich. You are so fortunate! This is wonderful! What a tremendous blessing."*

*The farmer softly replied, "Maybe so."*

*A few weeks later, the young son had his leg shattered while trying to break one of the wild horses.*

*The old man passing by again said, "This is so tragic!*

*Such a fine young man crippled and barely walking. His life is all but ruined. This is really awful. How tragic for you both. You don't deserve this terrible curse."*

*The farmer calmly replied, "Maybe so."*

*A few months later, the country went to war, and all the young men were called away to fight, including the son. All of them were killed in battle except for the farmer's son, who wasn't allowed at the front lines because of his broken leg.*

The story can go on and on, demonstrating that life's events can be judged as good or bad or they can be experienced without judgment and with a sense of grace instead. We really don't know what the future holds and what an event really means. Judging it, saying it's good or saying it's bad, is only pretending you know something you really don't; and getting fearful and upset about it is unjustified in the moment.

Judging from this place demonstrates a lack of faith in the Universe. Judging situations keeps you in constant conflict, fearing what "bad" thing is going to come your way next and hoping for something "good" to happen, when in truth none of us ever really knows for sure what an event means in our lives, especially not while it is happening.

Another example of this happened with a good friend of mine named Robert. Robert partnered with Jeffrey on a start-up business. A few months later, Jeffrey stole all of the company money, half of which was Robert's, and fled the state. At the time, it looked like a horrible situation for Robert; he was broke, he was full of worry, his company was bankrupt, and things looked pretty bleak.

Today if you ask Robert about it, he'll tell you it was one of the best things that ever happened to him in business because it led him to another line of work where he has prospered tremendously, far more than he ever would have in the other business. So judging a situation as bad isn't appropriate because you really don't know what the Universe is trying to do for you.

Every moment you have a choice. Who would you rather be like, the old neighbor who lives the emotional roller coaster of judgment or the farmer who lives life peacefully? Either way, the Universe is going to bring what it brings. You can choose to relate to these situations with fear, unrest, and resistance or with grace, peace, and acceptance.

When you decide you don't want to keep waking up to your judgmental nature and want to have more peace, you'll want to practice and master the following skill.

## FORGIVENESS

If you didn't judge, you would never need forgiveness. If you went through your life accepting others and situations as they are, you would likely never have anything to be upset about. Life would be always beautiful because you'd be in harmony with everything.

The problem is, you do judge, I judge, we all judge, and we all get upset. It's part of our humanness and our culture, but it is something we can improve upon greatly.

A woman came to see me after four years being divorced from her husband of 15 years. She told me she had been in and out of therapy for several years and had been working on getting over her ex-husband, the divorce, and all that came with that.

From what I could initially tell, she still seemed very sensitive, edgy, and judgmental about what had happened. At one point I asked her, "Have you ever worked with forgiveness?"

She snapped back with angry voice, "No. That son-of-a-bitch! He doesn't deserve it for what he did. I will never forgive him, nor will I ever talk to him again!"

I then asked her, "Where is he right now?"

"Hopefully suffering in hell!" she said.

I looked deeply into her eyes and asked her, "Who do you know, right now, who is suffering in hell?"

She paused for a very long time in silence and then began to cry. "I am," she said.

We often hold onto anger, hate, and resentment towards someone we think hurt us, believing that we are somehow punishing them or teaching them some kind of lesson. We sometimes think that if we forgive them, then we are giving in and losing. We think that if we forgive them, then they will have power over us and we will be inferior.

We often believe that forgiving them makes them right and us wrong. We say to ourselves, "He doesn't deserve to be forgiven. He doesn't deserve my love!" So instead, we hold our judgment, maintain our false pride, and slowly die inside.

Most people who offend you probably don't even have a clue that they have done anything. You may be boiling inside while they are skipping down the street whistling a cheery tune. Even if others have intentionally set out to cause you harm, the intention to do harm to another illustrates how deeply fearful and unconscious they are of themselves.

Never underestimate the power of fear. Someone who is acting from fear is someone who is not fully in their right mind. A fearful mind is not a clear-thinking mind. A fearful person is not aligned with their Soul. If you are in the practice of being resentful and angry, you are in no different mind than those who would cause you harm.

The degree and intensity of our fear can vary greatly. The degree to which we are in our fear determines our level of unconsciousness. Someone who is terrified is likely to be very unconscious of present-moment experience and is apt to make choices that can be very destructive to themselves and others. This person is likely to say and do things reactively without awareness of how it will affect himself or others. A person in fear is going to make mistakes that hurt others and himself.

A hurtful action can be looked at like a cough. The cough is only a symptom of a greater ailment. If someone has pneumonia and coughs around you, you wouldn't attack them in response. You would likely find compassion for them and their illness. A person in fear can be looked upon as someone with a spiritual ailment who is suffering from a lack of love and peace in their life.

As Jesus was nailed to the cross by a mob of people, He said, "Forgive them, Father, for they know not what they do" (Luke 23:44). If anyone had a right to be pissed off and hold a grudge, Jesus did; but He knew that those people who were doing Him physical harm were afraid and unconscious of their actions. He knew that they didn't know about love.

He knew that if He was to remain connected to the Spirit within Himself, He had to seek compassion and find forgiveness for those who were torturing His body. Jesus knew that peace and connection was found by connecting to the higher part of Himself within. He knew that the mob could take His body but not His peace of heart. He knew that the path and connection to God was through unconditional loving.

Forgiveness is the termination of resentment and hatred. It is letting go of guilt, whether it is your own or the guilt you place on another. It is the surrendering and undoing of judgment. Forgiveness is recognizing that someone is not defined by their actions.

It is the reinstatement of your unconditional loving perspective. Forgiveness is re-aligning your mind. It is looking past the unconscious mistake and fear to the innocence that lies within. It is returning your heart to a loving, peaceful place. Mark Twain said it beautifully, "Forgiveness is the fragrance a violet yields on the heel of the boot that crushed it."

Forgiveness is something that happens inside you. It is not necessary that you see the person face to face in order to forgive. There may be those whom you've held a long-standing resentment towards that are no longer around. You can still find forgiveness and make peace with that person inside yourself. Love is happening on the spiritual plane, not on the physical plane; it doesn't matter if someone is near or far, dead or alive. Love transcends the bounds of the physical world.

Part of practicing forgiveness is learning to let little things go by without the need to defend yourself or uphold your pride to others. It's about not being offended in the first place and, if you are, instantly letting go of it.

There are lots of people who would try to draw you into their drama and conflicts by subversively attacking or insulting you with words. Some may even talk behind your back. The path to peace is often best walked by not engaging in another's cheap drama of words. Letting it all roll off you is the wise way of handling toxic drama.

The quickest way to put this kind of fire out is by not giving it any fuel. Raise yourself above the pettiness of the little things. Stop judging those who seek petty conflict. If you let it go and find a way to love them, that is forgiveness and that is the way to remain at peace.

Forgiveness does not mean you stop making practical decisions with your life and your relationships. Just because you forgive a thief for stealing your purse or lawn mower doesn't mean you let him borrow the keys to your car. Forgiveness should not cause you to lose your good sense. You may forgive a thief for stealing from you and still show up in court to testify against him. Forgiving someone doesn't mean you don't protect yourself or others from the physical harm that person may inflict.

Don't confuse forgiving someone with condoning a behavior.

Forgiveness doesn't give someone a pass on the consequences of their actions. Forgiveness is about returning you to a peaceful and loving place inside yourself. It is about reconnecting you to that beautiful Soulful experience that brings you back into harmony with everything.

Forgiveness is the cornerstone to any enduring, healthy relationship. A relationship in which forgiveness is not practiced is diseased. A person who can't forgive their own judgments is diseased, and it will show up in all kinds of health problems, addictions, and so on.

The following is a practical method that may help you at times move toward forgiveness and peace.

## Forgiveness Practice

1. Be open for love to enter your heart. Ask Spirit to help you find peace.

2. Identify what it is that upset you. What happened?

3. Identify any judgments you have made about that person. How are they wrong?

4. Fully experience any emotional charge (anger, sadness, grief, etc.) and release it.

5. Ask yourself, *Were they coming from a loving space or a fearful space?*

6. Become aware that if they were coming from a fearful place, their choices would likely be irrational, unloving, and misguided.

7. Forgive them. (Example: I forgive you, _____. I recognize that you were afraid and doing the best you could with what you had in the moment.)

8. Find compassion for them. (Example: I understand what it is like to be in a fearful unloving space. I have been there myself, and I too have caused harm to another or have been capable of harming another.)

9. Send them loving thoughts and/or pray for them. (Example: I ask Spirit to help you find love and peace within your heart and also within mine.)

## SELF-FORGIVENESS

I suggest you follow the same process of forgiveness for yourself. The simple act of judging another is an act worthy of self-forgiveness. The act of judging one's self as wrong or unworthy is also an act worthy of self-forgiveness. Holding resentment against yourself is equally harmful to holding resentment toward another.

We are all our own worst critics. So practice forgiving yourself and others as quickly as you recognize fear and upset coming up inside of you. You will find life and relationships a lot easier and a lot more fulfilling.

## CHAPTER 12

# Give Generously and Receive Graciously

*Before giving, the mind of the giver is happy;*
*while giving, the mind of the giver is made peaceful;*
*and having given, the mind of the giver is uplifted.*

**—Buddha**

If you feel unfulfilled because you think you are not getting what you need out of your relationships with others, the problem possibly lies in what you are not giving.

Many of us go into relationships with a misaligned mindset when it comes to giving and receiving. We're too occupied with thoughts like: *What am I going to get out of this?* or *What does he or she have to offer me?* We may also struggle, bargain, and manipulate to get what we think we want and need from other people, oftentimes with little thought as to what is right for them.

It's easy to get so wrapped up in ourselves that we don't stop for a moment to think if what we are doing is beneficial to the ones we love. Even at times when we think we are giving to another, we're actually doing it for some ego-serving reason we don't really want to acknowledge, which isn't true giving. This mindset is what has to change in order for us to feel fulfilled.

When you give someone a gift or do them a favor, you are usually coming from one of two perspectives. The first perspective is,

"I am lacking something in my life, I want something from you, and I am willing to make a trade." This is the ego perspective.

The second is, "I have abundance in my life and want to share it with you because I want you to have abundance as well." This is the Soulful perspective.

## GIVING WITH EXPECTATIONS

Have you ever stopped to observe what perspective you are coming from when you offer something to someone else? This can be a confronting question to ask yourself the next time you do a favor for someone.

If you give to someone with an expectation or attachment to a particular result, it is not a gift. It is a deal you are trying to make without the conscious agreement of the other person. It is not a gift but rather bait with a hook inside, trying to catch and manipulate someone to do what you want. I see couples do this with one another all the time.

One woman I worked with would do all kinds of things for her boyfriend. She would buy him gifts, clean his house, do his laundry, and prepare beautiful and elaborate meals. She would spend nearly an entire day cooking, setting candles, decorating the house, chilling wine, making dessert, and on and on. She was always setting a scene for something. Everything was choreographed perfectly.

Except for one thing—he didn't know his part. When he came home and didn't deliver what she was expecting from him, she became hurt, angry, and resentful. All of her gifts were given conditionally from a place of neediness and want. Her real excitement from giving came from the hope that he would give her the kind of attention she wanted in return. Every time, she was left disappointed, hurt, and unsatisfied. She did this with several boyfriends over several years all with the same results.

This way of "giving to get" comes from a fearful place within you. If you have ever tried getting someone to love you by doing things for them, you know how frustrating and scary it can be. It feels like there is an empty, painful hole inside you that you believe someone else's attention will fill. The scary part of all this is, you are relying on another for your inner well-being, and he might not give you what you need. But … the scariest part is, he might give you what you think you need, but that empty, painful hole will still be there inside you. Another person can't give you what your Soul craves because your Soul craves giving.

When the shoe is on the other foot and someone is trying to make a deal for your affection by giving you something with strings attached, it can be equally disturbing. If you've ever had someone desperately trying to get your love and attention by giving you things, you know it can feel like you are being scammed. If you have ever had someone proclaim their love for you from this space, you know it doesn't feel like love at all. You sense on a deeper level that he really doesn't offer you love; it feels more like he is trying to covertly steal something away from you.

When someone does you a favor and then sits at your feet and begs like a starving puppy for your attention, the favor certainly doesn't feel like a favor. It feels more like a trap. When someone is in this place, they experience love like it is a possession that can be held on to and hoarded. They are a bottomless pit of neediness that no one can fill but themselves. The problem is, they are unwilling or unknowing about how to give themselves the love they so desperately want from you.

### GIVING FROM NEED

There is a certain amount of satisfaction we all can receive when we get something in the form of a gift from another. But is it really as deeply rewarding as you expected it to be? There are people I know who have been given everything their entire lives who are miserably unhappy with their lives. They have been given money, homes, cars, fine educations, jobs, everything, including love, but they still don't feel satisfied. They seem to always be looking for the next thing or the next person to give them something more that will bring them happiness.

The next thing and the next person comes and goes, again and again, yet these people never seem to get those inner needs met. It is like waiting on a check to arrive in the mail; they go to the mailbox everyday and look inside, but it never ever shows up.

The difference in dealing and true giving lies in the intent. A dealer is willing to give up to a point but only if they think they will get something they want from someone to replenish his stores.

When you're playing the dealer role, you may be willing to trade something sacred in order to get what you think you need from someone else. You may offer your money, your time, your home, sex, or jeopardize your integrity in some way, all in an effort to get that "certain something" that you think they have that will make you satisfied. This kind of trade has been called "making a deal with the devil."

The classic example is the young, beautiful, Hollywood starlet hooking up with the tired, old, wealthy film producer. She's got beauty, charm, and sex appeal that excite him; he's got experience, money, and influence to help her career—so they make an unspoken deal to be together. But it's a lie because the love and connection isn't there. We've all probably seen marriages between dealers in our lives; it is easy to tell those because there is no light in their eyes for one another. It's because they are disconnected from their Souls.

Have you ever been someone who has said, "I gave and gave until it hurt"? This comes from the same mindset of "giving to get." The hurt comes from not getting what you were bargaining for. When in this space, you believe that love is limited—love is something that will eventually run out if you give too much. This is the voice that says you can't be too generous and loving towards other people because eventually you will deplete your stores and have nothing for yourself. When you're in this ego mindset, you can never feel at peace, no matter what you get in return, because it will eventually not be enough. There may be moments of satisfaction, but in a short time your ego will need more.

It may appear on the surface that the dealer is being loving and giving, but love isn't present. Fear and need are present. So when you are a dealer, there is little satisfaction in the act of being of service to others because the action is not authentic. There may be excitement from the anticipation of getting what you want, but nothing meaningful results from the act itself. The only reward for you comes if the receiver responds according to your desire. If the deal doesn't go through, which it ultimately never does, disappointment, pain, and resentment occur.

## GIVING WITH LOVE

You have likely always suspected deep down that no one else could give you what you needed to make you feel whole, but you may have kept on trying because it appears more tangible than finding love within yourself. This is understandable because this is what we are so often told by the outside world. It doesn't work, never has and never will. The reason your ego loves looking for someone else to give you happiness is because it takes the pressure and responsibility off you to make the necessary changes in yourself. When they fail to give it to you, then you have someone to blame for the relationship not working out and you not being fulfilled by it.

Love doesn't work the same way as most systems do in our society, and this is how many of us get confused. For instance, it is possible for someone else to give you so much money that you will never lack money for your entire lifetime. However, it is not possible for someone else to give you so much love that you will never feel a lack of love again. Winston Churchill said, "We make a living by what we get; we make a life by what we give."

The love given from others can be wonderful, but it is never enough to deeply satisfy the desires of the Soul. The Soul wants to give, the Soul has to be giving for you to feel love and peace. The forces of love work in opposition to rational worldly thought: in order to have more love, you have to give away more love. This only makes sense from a spiritual perspective. The love that deeply satisfies you will not be the love given to you by someone else; it will be the love you have given to someone else.

A gift is only as good as the love behind it. A gift of love is not something you can hold in your hand or see with your eyes. It is not in a diamond or a toy. These things can be symbols of your love; but of themselves, they hold no value. The symbol in itself is meaningless unless real love is conveyed along with it.

A man can give a woman an expensive diamond ring and not share his love with her. A mother can give a child a brand new toy, and it can be an empty, meaningless experience if love is not shared. Kahlil Gibran said, "You give but little when you give of your possessions. It is when you give of yourself that you truly give."

A gift of any kind, no matter how small, can have great meaning and significance to both the giver and receiver if the message "I care" accompanies that gift. That message is what truly matters to most of us.

Love costs nothing, and yet it is the most valuable commodity on the planet. We all have immeasurable quantities of it, yet we can hoard it like breadcrumbs in a prison camp, only doling it out to other people on rare occasions.

From time to time in life, you meet someone you feel comfortable enough being with that you are uninhibited in expressing yourself. This sense of safety and trust allows you permission to let your love flow safely. When this happens, you tend to shower this person with love and affection. In the moment, you have little concern about getting it back. It doesn't matter because it felt so great giving it away.

Maya Angelou said, "I have found that among its other benefits, giving liberates the soul of the giver." The more you give, the more love you feel for another and the better you feel about yourself. That is how love works, and it can work that way with anyone, including you—if you allow yourself to go for it.

Quite often, a major part of the pain involved in breaking off a romantic relationship comes from not having someone to give to any longer. I have found that when someone has a lot of loving people in their life to give and share with, they are far less troubled by a breakup with a romantic partner. Because they have other outlets where they can express their love, there is not the neediness and desperation for that one and only person with whom they can share love. It is the pain of not giving our love to someone that hurts the most. This is why we should be conscious and give love to everyone, every time we can.

A woman in her early forties came to see me about her life's relationship problems. Her father had left her mother when she was young, and from that day forward she carried a wound from that. She told me about how every man she was with eventually left her, and how she would never let herself really love anyone fully because she was afraid they would leave. The last man she was with left her and told her he was leaving because her heart was closed, and he wanted to share a loving relationship with her.

A loving relationship is what she really desires for herself but couldn't express because of her fear of being left again. She held onto her love and affection and by doing so drove men away. She thought she was protecting herself from pain, but she was really creating exactly what she most feared.

## SHARING YOUR GIFT

Anytime you think that giving love is going to cost you something or bind you in some way, you are not coming from the Soul. If you don't expect anything in return, you have nothing to fear by giving your love away. If it doesn't matter to you how they react or respond, you have nothing to lose and everything to gain. You can be giving and loving towards anyone just because it feels right for you. Love is its own reward.

By giving a gift to another with love, you are actually giving yourself the greatest gift you can get. When you share your love with someone, you are feeding your Soul. When coming from a place of pure love, you need nothing in return. Helping another or loving another in any manner is a gift to yourself.

Love expands—the more you give, the more you have to give. It swells inside you like a sponge with no limits. The more you squeeze it out, the bigger it gets the next time. Giving is the reward in itself.

My great-uncle Bill Newman was one of the happiest people I have ever known. He lived his life from a perspective of service to others, and I believe that is what made his life so full. He always had something to give another. Sometimes it would be a simple compliment, but it always seemed sincere and given without expectation.

One time around the Thanksgiving holiday, my family was gathered at my parents' home for dinner. I was telling my mother that I was looking at buying a new watch, something nice that I could wear to formal occasions.

Bill overheard our conversation and asked, "What style are you looking for?"

I happened to glance at his watch and said, "I don't know. Something like the one you have on. That one is really nice."

Right then he took his watch off his arm and said, "Here, take it. It's yours."

I was caught completely by surprise. I began to say *No* because I felt like that was too generous, but I couldn't because I could see how happy he was about giving it to me. That day, he gave me much more than a watch. He gave me a lesson I have never forgotten.

If you aren't getting what you want in a situation, turn the mirror on yourself and look to see if you are giving what you are hoping to get. If you want more affection from someone, be more affectionate. If you want more love in your life, give more love to others. If you want more openness and honesty from others, be more open and honest with others. If you want prosperity, assist others in becoming prosperous.

Once you get over the initial fear, you will find that by giving and being of service to others, you will not be concerned about what is missing in your own life. You will feel a fullness, a completeness that can come from no other source but that of giving.

Being of service may mean letting someone pull in front of you in traffic. It may mean stopping and holding the door open for someone. It could be a card to someone telling them you were thinking of them. Anything that you can do for another as a favor with no expectation or desire for personal gain is being of service.

The test is, would you do this favor or give this gift if they never knew you did it? If you would and would feel good about it, your heart is in alignment with the Soul.

## RECEIVING LOVE

Some people are great at giving to others, but they are lousy at receiving from others. I've frequently noticed when I've complimented people, they will not openly accept my compliment. They don't reject it, but they don't really accept it either. They brush it off and say something like "Ah, nah, I wish I was that good" or "Thanks, but I am not as good as I want to be" or something like that. They don't fully embrace the honor and gift that I have attempted to give them.

The same thing goes when offering to help someone by giving them something material. They resist receiving it. Just the other day I saw an older man struggling to lift some fence posts onto his truck. These posts weren't extremely heavy, but they were unwieldy because they were bundled together. I offered, "I'm glad to help you if you would like some help with those."

He said, "Nah, thanks. I think I can get it," as he dropped the load on the tailgate, jamming his finger.

I wished him a good day and walked on. I thought to myself, *I can be just like that man, denying the help I obviously need while at the same time denying a great opportunity to connect with another person.*

The problem many of us can have with receiving gifts, compliments, and help from others is our ego gets in the way. We can be too prideful. We don't believe we are worthy of gifts or compliments, so we have a hard to accepting them and hearing them. We don't accept help when we need it because we don't want to appear vulnerable or weak. But receiving an offering doesn't make you a "taker" in the selfish sense of the word. This mindset shuts down the opportunity to share a meaningful connection with someone. It denies them the joy of giving, and it denies you the same joy.

There is nothing selfish about being an open and grateful receiver. In fact, being a good receiver is a generous act. By being a gracious receiver, you honor someone who is giving to you. By thankfully accepting their offer, you are in essence giving to them as well. If you deny their gift or offering, you deny them the joyful feeling they will have from being of service to you. By denying their offering, you may shut the door on the free-flowing exchange of love and connection. By accepting their offering, you allow them to share and replenish their Soul.

Your acceptance is also an act of giving; you are giving them the space to express their love and appreciation for you. This is why we love our pets so much. They are gracious receivers of our love and affection. We can love them and give them affection 24 hours a day, and they are almost always open to receiving. We feel connected to our pets because they allow us express ourselves without resistance. They freely accept our gifts.

So the next time someone offers something to you, think twice before you reject it. If appropriate, accept it enthusiastically, give him a heartfelt thank you, and open yourself up to a new level of sharing. If it helps, imagine yourself as a dog or cat that rolls around in the affection and appreciation of another.

By welcoming the offerings of others, you help create a spiritual wealth that enriches the lives of both the giver and the receiver. Once you've experienced what spiritual wealth is all about, you will know that no other kind of wealth has any real value.

## CHAPTER 13

# Step Up into Greater Connection

*He who knows others is wise.*
*He who knows himself is enlightened.*

—Lao Tzu

*A*lthough most of us start out in the world as children with an enlightened, Soul-connected way of experiencing those around us, we lose touch with it. Because the messages of the world turn us inside out, we most often have to go through a process of experiences or a series of life stages before we are ready to return to that centered mindset.

The path to getting there is a bit different for each of us, but there are many similarities on our paths. The real measure of where we are on the path can be based on how much joy we are experiencing in life and how full we feel inside our hearts.

### FIVE PHASES OF INNER RELATIONSHIP GROWTH

Below are the relationship phases, or perspectives, we all experience. These may help you understand where you have been and where you are going, or where you want to be going.

#### ✦ The Innocent Child

The perspective on life you had as a child is probably much different from the one you have now. However, that childhood perspective is still inside you somewhere; and if you've spent much time with children, you're probably fresh with the experience.

One of the biggest joys about being with children is they can show you the way back to that place of wonder and mystery where everything seems beautiful, interesting, and lovable. Kids can remind you how to see the world through enlightened eyes.

My two-year-old nephew lights up at the sight of a dog walking down the sidewalk. He looks at it like it's an old friend he hasn't seen in years. He also loves to go to the coffee shop where he gets to see new faces, say hello, and make new friends. With a fresh, clear view and without bias or judgment, he is experiencing the world with an innocent mindset.

In many ways, he seems much closer and connected to the realm of Spirit than I am at most times of my day. At his age, he's mostly unencumbered by the false teachings of the world. He sees relationships in their simplistic essence. There are no real rules to follow, no dating games to play, no form or structure to adhere to, few expectations to meet, no pressure to get married, no right or wrong way to be in a relationship, no commitments to keep—just the freedom to be who he is, where he is in the present moment.

Most of us are, unfortunately, heavily encumbered in our minds and often have to let go of a lot of things to get to this place. But it's the transformation of mind that returns us to a place of peace.

And this is not a new idea.

Jesus taught his disciples, "Unless you change and become like little children, you will never enter the kingdom of Heaven" (Matthew 18:3). Jesus was telling them they needed to change their perspectives, return to their enlightened and non-judgmental state, and start to see the world through eyes of the innocent child within themselves.

And Lao Tzu in the *Tao Te Ch'ing* says, "Being in the stream of the universe, ever true and unswerving, become as a little child once more."

But what soon happens takes us all away from this childhood sense of wonder. We start to learn the false teachings of the world. Our pristine hearts and minds begin to get polluted. Our natural, enlightened state gets destroyed. We begin to learn how relationships are "supposed" to be. We get a program of how we "should" live our lives, conduct our relationships. And this puts us into another experience.

## ✦ The Naïve Beginner

If you're in this phase, usually you have a perspective typical of early adulthood and one of youthful inexperience with relationships. From here, you see the world and how to be in relationships based mostly on what others have taught you. In this state of mind, you rely on fantasy, unconsciously considering the Cinderella story and other romantic tales as models for your relationships. You become idealistic, have a low level of self-awareness, and believe that love will come to you in the form of one perfect person.

You are mostly unaware of your self-destructive and relationship-harming behaviors. You're usually unwed—hoping someone will arrive soon to change that, or newly wed. You take little or no responsibility for your own happiness, believing that happiness comes to you from outside you. You will also blame others for your troubles and unhappiness.

You likely hold on to your love and affection, waiting to direct it to "one special, deserving person," thus creating love-anemic social circles or loneliness within yourself. You greatly fear being alone and are unaware that you have an ego-centered "What's in it for me?" world view. The young woman looking for her "Knight in Shining Armor" or "Prince Charming" or the young man seeking "Miss Perfect" to make her or him happy is typical of this perspective.

At some point, this perspective will likely be shattered to pieces, and you may move to the next phase.

## ✦ The Wounded Veteran

More experienced than the Naïve Beginner, you've had broken relationships, busted fantasies, and suffered some wounds from the experiences. From this mindset, you've lived the truth that your dreams don't always equate to reality. Maybe you have experienced divorce or been involved in serious relationships that did not work out as you had planned. You have some sense of self-awareness yet still believe love and happiness is associated with acceptance from others, or the right partner, or perhaps changing your current partner.

If single, you likely are still seeking another "Prince Charming" or "Miss Perfect" to make you happy or have become bitter and given up on dating. You continue to carry glamorous romantic illusions about love and relationships even though your experiences have proven contradictory to your beliefs.

You have a resistance to emotional intimacy and protect yourself with fear of further wounding. You carry hidden, unhealed wounds from past relationships and have some awareness of those wounds but are not actively working toward healing them. You rarely take responsibility for your relationship difficulties, fear being alone or without a partner, and likely repeat destructive relationship patterns over and over again. If you're someone who has been married multiple times or your relationships typically end painfully and dramatically while thinking your pain is "their" fault, you're likely in a Veteran perspective.

If you are waking up and realizing that your relationships are not working, you may make the choice to do something about it. If so, you move on to the next phase. If not—you stay stuck here.

## ✦ The Defeated Seeker

This experience is similar to that of a Veteran but with an awareness that what you've been doing in relationships is not working anymore. Your ego has suffered many defeats, and you've realized there may be something more out there.

From this place, you have a much greater sense of self-awareness. You question the status quo, you question your old belief systems, and you've awakened to the realization that your fantasies are not reality.

So you're now looking for truth.

You carry unhealed wounds and work diligently to learn and grow in order to heal them. You are actively attempting to take responsibility for your own actions/reactions to situations and are realizing that you are responsible for your own happiness. You are committed to improving your life and relationships; you want outside help and education. You attempt to avoid destructive, toxic relationship situations while building loving social circles around yourself. You may carry many other fears, but you work towards overcoming them as opposed to avoiding them.

The most defining characteristic of this perspective is your active pursuit of learning, healing your own inner pain, and taking responsibility for your own well-being. Those who spend time reading self-help books, attending workshops/groups, pursuing counseling/therapy, exploring and deepening spiritual awareness, and exploring themselves trying to obtain or maintain some real inner peace are typical of seekers.

As a diligent and committed seeker of knowledge and healing, you will likely be moving towards the next perspective.

## ✦ The Enlightened Heart

This perspective comes from a place of being awake, informed, centered in yourself and your inner knowing. It is the ability to see the world through the eyes of a child with the wisdom of a mature adult. You are a Seeker who has found the experience of Inner Peace and has the inner skills to return to it. You've connected to Spirit; you know the experience.

From this place, you've experienced a profound sense of your own inner healing. You continue to learn, and you seek to help others heal and grow. You don't rely on fantasy as a relationship model and do experience relationships in the present moment.

You have an expansive awareness of your inner self, have a strong connection to intuition, are open to giving and receiving love while experiencing a deep love for yourself and others. You understand love comes from a divine Source within and seek time to be alone to connect to that place.

You realize a romantic partner is someone to share love and life with, yet is not the source of your happiness. You take responsibility for your actions/reactions and, though not perfect, can often see where you aren't expressing love and are able to make self-corrections. You're not dependent on another person for your emotional and spiritual well-being; you understand the dynamics of fear and un-conditional love.

You're comfortable with emotional intimacy, carry a fullness of heart, and genuinely want all others to experience the same. You feel a loving connection towards the world; you see the beings of the world as your community.

These phases do not classify you or anyone else into one group. No one is all of one or the other. All perspectives can show up at different times in different situations for any of us. The general progression of consciousness and maturity from the Naïve to the Enlightened is not an event like graduating from one grade level in school to another.

As you grow and progress, you may leave behind many delusions, but you may also realize that you are still attached to some. You may jump ahead, having moments of enlightened wisdom and Soul-connectedness, seeing the world as perfectly beautiful for a time, and then fall back, thinking you need to be loved by some person or you cannot continue to live well. This is the nature of the struggle between the ego and your Soul. Growth is a process, not an event.

Enlightenment with relationships does not mean you're finished learning. It really only means you've awakened to what does not work and have begun to glimpse and experience what could be if you continue to practice what you now know. All of this is an effort to experience the one thing we all ultimately want.

## TRANSCENDENCE THROUGH LOVE

The ultimate goal in your relationships with everyone and everything is to experience love. The transcendent experience occurs when you rise above the thought complications of worldly situations and feel the connection with Spirit. Simply put, it's the experience of deep inner peace and connection, the experience of Oneness that comes from unconditional loving.

It is a sense of completeness, wholeness, gratitude, and heartfelt affection. It is the experience of love that fills you up and lifts you above all worldly concerns. It can happen when another is either present with you or present in your mind.

When you experience transcendent love, you will know it because nothing else will seem more important than that moment. It can occur when you think of someone with nothing but affirmation, appreciation, respect, and honor for him with no need or want for anything in return.

If you have even a glimmer of hostility or judgment within you about this person, transcendence comes at the moment you release that and experience only love. It's the same inner experience as "falling in love" without the dependence and fear of losing it.

One of the primary symptoms is tears of joy, which may at times also feel like a mix of sadness and joy; but it's more a fullness of heart than an emptiness of heart. One of the best ways I've found to create this experience is to think about someone close to me for whom I have a great deal of appreciation.

I often ask clients to take private alone time to write a letter to someone they love—telling them why they love them, what they appreciate about them, and the qualities that makes them such a good friend. If you try this exercise, you will likely be moved towards the transcendence experience.

Another thing you can do is tell your friend face to face, which may be scary; but if you do it without any expectations or wants from them, you may be brought to this experience of loving connection.

It is often hard for us to tell people we love them and honor them. We have a fear inside of us that we will be rejected, or they will not accept us and what we are saying, or something. But this fear is the obstacle that keeps us from experiencing connection in our lives. This experience of transcendence—Heaven, bliss, love, or whatever you want to call it—happens when we express inner affection for those around us. It can be as simple as a loving thought about another that can bring us to this place.

An example of one of my spiritually connected, transcendent moments came when I sat quietly and thought about a long-time friend who had been in my life for 37 years. I thought about how he has been there for me, loved me, kept in contact with me over many years, and been an honorable man around me. My thoughts and appreciation for him and our friendship brought me to tears of bliss. He wasn't around, except in my mind, yet I felt mystically connected with our Souls.

There are some outer things you can do and qualities you can embrace that will bring your relationship experiences with others much more into alignment. However, the transcendent experience is something that happens within you. Unlike most of what you've learned about relationships, the basis of a relationship is happening inside you and has little or nothing to do with the other person. When you align with what brings you peace, it brings your relationships with others that much closer to transcendence.

## EIGHT ESSENTIAL PRACTICES

Although the transcendent experience is beyond the physical realm, there are some qualities you can practice that help build the foundation for arriving at this spiritual place. These qualities are also essential for creating a space for love and connection to grow between you and another.

### ✦ Integrity

Integrity is about honesty and keeping aligned with your internal code that brings you peace. It comes from keeping your word and your agreements.

It is about congruency of intention with action. It's when you mean what you say and do what you say. It's about matching what goes on inside you with what goes on outside you. It's about speaking your truth and living that truth.

Demonstrating dishonesty or unreliability creates a space where fear and apprehension flourish, which creates a block to connection. An example of not being in integrity is when your Inner Voice tells you to leave an unhappy situation, yet you do nothing.

When you are living with integrity, you will be at peace because living in this manner is the foundation for mutually loving, respectful relationships. It's also the foundation on which you grow in your own self-loving. You are solid, full, complete, and without regret, guilt, or need for apology. If you like someone and your Inner Voice wants you to express it, being in integrity with yourself is expressing it.

Being someone who keeps their word is demonstrating that you are someone that others can trust. Being someone who is trustworthy creates a level of safety in the relationship, and this sense of safety helps to remove fears others may be carrying. Without fear, others are apt to drop their guard; you are both brought much closer to the experience of mutual connection.

A common situation where people often reveal a level of integrity occurs where meetings are concerned. For example, if you and I agree that you are going to pick me up at 7:00 P.M. to go to a dinner party, you have made a pact with me and yourself to be there on time. Your being in integrity with me means you will be there at 7:00 P.M. Not 6:45, not 7:30, but 7:00.

If you arrive early thinking it is better to be early than late, you are still out of integrity. I may not be ready or may have another commitment, and your early arrival upsets or stresses my schedule. And you agreed to be there at 7:00. If you arrive late, it also sends the message that you do not value my time or that you are not reliable.

Being early or late can create a rift in the relationship. It may be subtle and get overlooked, but any break in integrity can create a separation, a little break in trust that allows a hint of doubt and fear to slip between us. This separation occurs between you and me and you and you.

On the other hand, if you arrive at my door at 7:00, it sends a message to me that you are someone I can rely on, that you are someone who cares about my time and has respect for me, as well as yourself. It maintains the wholeness of the relationship and lifts it up to another level. Being someone of high integrity removes fear from others because they feel safe around you. This is invaluable for creating and clearing the space for love to flourish.

Although this situation may be a small issue of importance compared to many others, any break in integrity, whether it be with you and someone else or an agreement you make with yourself, can disrupt the wholeness of the relationship. If it happens over and over, it can destroy a relationship.

Another common area in romantic relationships that test one's integrity is centered around commitment and fidelity. Depending on which research study you look at, over half of married men and women will cheat on their spouses during their marriage. Even if your partner does not know you are lying or cheating, you do. This not only seriously damages the relationship with a partner, it seriously damages the relationship you have with yourself.

If you do not want to be married or monogamous, don't be—stay in integrity with yourself, live from that place, be honest with yourself and others. Life will be a whole lot easier and much more peaceful.

## *The six steps for maintaining integrity:*

1. **MAKE FEWER AGREEMENTS AND COMMITMENTS.** Be willing to say, "No, I am not comfortable committing to that at this point." Do not over-commit yourself!

2. **ONLY MAKE AGREEMENTS YOU FULLY INTEND TO KEEP.** If your heart really is not in it or you do not believe you are doing the right thing, you are not likely to follow through with passion. Live your life doing what you really want to do!

3. **RENEGOTIATE IF NECESSARY.** Give yourself permission to make adjustments to the original agreement you made with yourself or another as needed. Negotiate an alternative arrangement that is win-win for everyone whenever possible.

4. **WRITE IT DOWN.** Anytime you commit to something or someone and you do not want to forget it, write it down someplace where you will see it. Help yourself be timely with your agreement.

5. **BE RESPONSIBLE WHEN YOU ERR.** Everyone makes mistakes, but not everyone takes ownership of them. Be someone who does, and make it right whenever possible. Clean up your part of the mess, and mend all wounds as best you can.

6. **FORGIVE YOURSELF AND OTHERS.** Maintaining integrity is often a process of trial and error. You will make mistakes, and so will others. You may not be able to forget, but you can forgive. Bring yourself back to your loving center as soon as you can.

When you are not living from a place of integrity, you are not aligned with the Universe and you will not be truly at peace. When you are not living with integrity, your life will be chaotic and full of upset.

Being in integrity is about speaking your truth and living your truth even though others may not like it. It is living your life in such a way that you do not need to lie to protect yourself. It is living life and being who you are without apology.

Being in integrity with Spirit is about listening to what your Inner Voice is telling you and following that with your life.

## ✦ Accountability

As mentioned briefly earlier, accountability is being responsible and taking ownership for your actions. It is also about being available to the relationship by being considerate and mindful of another. It is behaving in such a way that you are returned to integrity and wholeness when you have lost it. It is about owning your part in a given situation whether it is being honored for something well done or being criticized for a screw up. It usually is a lot harder to take the heat for screwing something up than it is to take credit for something done well, but accountability is about embracing whatever is yours.

Accountability is about owning your feelings, thoughts, and actions. Because your actions are not always perfect, you will make mistakes, circumstances will change, and agreements will be broken. Being available to correct them whenever possible is what gets you back to integrity, which means you have to be there, stand up, and take care of whatever you are responsible for messing up.

Using the previous example, say you are 45 minutes late in picking me up for dinner. I have not heard from you. I am getting upset and even a bit worried. You finally show up and give me a long excuse list, "I'm sorry. It's not my fault. I was on a phone call at work with a friend who needed help; I meant to call you but couldn't get off the phone. The traffic was horrible. My car was low on gas, so I had to stop." And so on.

This is not accountability, and I am not likely going to fullheartedly accept this apology; it is empty. But this is what many people do. The situation gets brushed off in order to avoid conflict. Yet it does not work towards creating connection; it destroys it because it lacks full truth.

This kind of behavior creates suspicion and distrust. It blocks intimacy because it says to another, "I cannot be trusted in the relationship. I am not solid." The inner conflict and separation is there, whether it gets voiced or not. Deep inside me, a flag of caution drops out, and the door of openheartedness begins to close.

And a similar thing begins to happen inside you.

This lack of accountability destroys connections. It also works to diminish your own self-esteem because you are not handling yourself in a loving way. You know you have messed up, and you know you are not doing what it takes to make things right again. If you were, you would be showing up in a way that brings you peace, not conflict.

To show me that you were accountable, you could have called me and said, "I'm running very late. It's totally my fault; I screwed up and didn't plan very well. I understand what it's like to be waiting for someone. You probably think I'm a flake, but I'm generally not. I want to make it up to you. What can I do?"

I might say, "Ah, it's no big deal," because I do not want to create a conflict.

This would give you the chance to respond with, "It *is* a big deal. I don't want this to come between us. Seriously, what do you need help with?"

Then I could say, "Okay, you're right! I want to work on my lawn for 45 minutes on Saturday, and you can help if you want. We will start at 10 A.M.!"

You agree and show up on Saturday at 10 A.M. and entertain me while we weed my lawn. By being available to show up, correct your actions, and making amends for them, I am much more likely to leave the door for connection open. In addition, you are likely to feel much more whole within yourself because you have returned yourself to integrity.

The journalist Sidney J. Harris said, "We have not passed that subtle line between childhood and adulthood until...we have stopped saying, 'It got lost,' and say, 'I lost it.'" This honest kind of ownership builds trust.

However, when you are coming from the ego mindset, you cannot stand to be wrong. You fear that if you admit a mistake or own up to it, you will lose something valuable or be rejected by those around you. In most cases the opposite is true—if you do not own up to it and be accountable for your actions, others will know it or sense it, and the connection will be lost. Or at least you will know, and the connection will still be lost within you.

### ✦ Commitment to Love

There is one commitment that trumps all others, and this one is your commitment to love. This commitment is bigger and more important to your sense of inner well-being than any living arrangement, any job commitment, marriage commitment, or contract.

This is a spiritual commitment to see and experience the divinity in another, no matter what the circumstances are at the time. When the validity of any other commitment is in question, the commitment to love shall be the fall back. When all other commitments are breaking down, you should always return to your commitment to be loving.

The only place I have seen this commitment even partially discussed or promoted is in traditional wedding vows where you might say, "I take you to be my husband/wife, to love and cherish you, as long as we both shall live." The most important part of this is "to love and cherish you, as long as we both shall live." Many people get hung up on the "I take you to be my husband/wife" and forget about or misunderstand the supreme importance of the rest of it.

It is fine to stay committed to the marriage; but without a commitment to love one another, the staying together part is just window dressing. Without the experience of love in any relationship, the other commitments are essentially meaningless. Even if a marriage ends in divorce, it still is a spiritually sound practice to love and cherish your ex-partner.

This marriage vow to love and cherish is made to your husband or wife, but what about the rest of the people in your life? Could you commit to love and cherish them as well?

The Soul-connected perspective on love is unconditional towards everyone. "Unconditional" means "no matter what happens." Loving another unconditionally means you agree to find your love for another no matter what he or she does or says. There is no "I love you, but ____" with unconditional love. It is "I love you." And that is that. What he is doing or not doing, whether the relationship is working or not are other issues to be worked out; but those issues don't have to affect your commitment to find love for another.

Finding love for someone can be difficult at times for sure, especially when someone has betrayed you or is attempting to do you harm. This is why the commitment to love unconditionally is so important. You do not love another unconditionally to only benefit him. You do it to bring you to peace, to reconnect you with the Soul. Your loving another benefits you as much as or more than anyone else.

The commitment to love can be an unspoken one you make not only to a romantic partner in good times, but to everyone in all times.

What if you made a vow to love all others? Perhaps it would look something like this:

> I commit to overcome MY inner obstacles in order to love you under any and all circumstances: when you are happy, when you are troubled, when you make mistakes, when you betray me, when you are sick, when you are rich or poor, when you are addicted, when you are rude, when you are my adversary, when we are fighting, when you need to leave my presence, when I need to leave yours, when we can no longer live together or be friends or be married, when we can no longer enjoy sex, when we can no longer share time, and even when I think I don't want to love you any more—I will find that place in my Soul that will.

The most critical part of committing to love another or ourselves is the willingness to overcome our own inner obstacles that keep us from that loving place.

This is the place where most people fail because they are not willing to face the fear or pride and do the inner work required to get past their own obstacles. They are not willing to set down their ego's pride and move through their fears in order to love without conditions.

But this is where the real growth occurs.

Whether it is going to therapy, attending support groups, or deepening a spiritual practice, don't quit when you start to see what you do not like about yourself in the mirror of truth. Facing your own inner obstacles is where the real work in a relationship takes place, and it is something only you can do.

Whether or not you have made a commitment to a marriage, a monogamous relationship, living together, a business partnership, or friendship, these worldly commitments are secondary to your commitment to love.

If you commit yourself to loving as first priority, all of your secondary commitments will take care of themselves.

The form of life situations will change, relationships will change because that is what happens; but your inner peace will not if you stay committed to loving through those changes. By loving, you are connected to something much bigger than the circumstances of life.

### ✦ Introspection

To stay connected to your enlightened Soul, you regularly take time to look within yourself to see how you are relating in the world. If a conflict arises, instead of reacting and blaming, you take an inventory of your thoughts, feelings, attitudes, and behavior.

Instead of looking for all the reasons you are right and the other person is wrong, it is best to first look at where you might be off track. It's best to look within and be with what's going on inside you. The questions you may ask yourself are: *How am I affecting this situation? What is my part? Am I responsible; if so, where? Am I being loving? How can I make it better? What can I do to return this situation to peace?*

By taking the time to be with yourself and reflect on the situation, you are much better able to determine where your responsibility may lie. From a place of introspection, you can decide the next most loving approach to take.

## ✦ Expansion

Expansion is stretching and increasing your ability to love. If you don't have enough love in your life, your container is too small. And your container is your own personal box, your comfort zone that you are used to living within.

In order to expand it so you can hold more, you have to push through some fears and overcome your limiting beliefs. You have to take risks and take a step further out in your relationships than you have in the past. It's been said, "If you keep doing what you've been doing, you'll keep getting what you've been getting." This is why you have to expand yourself.

Have you heard of growing pains?

Expansion will cause growing pains because you are stretching yourself psychologically beyond what you are used to now.

In order to expand, you may need to seek some help; this is why people go to therapy. A good therapist, life coach, group, or spiritual teacher can help you push through your own walls that are confining you to a life that is less than what you desire.

In my case, I needed a team of experts working for several years to help me get through some of my blocks. I attended 12-step groups, men's groups, therapy, seminars, and everything I could find that could teach me. It all helped, and I'm still working at it. Staying centered takes regular practice.

In order to expand, you have to find your sense of adventure and be willing to face your fears. You don't have to face them all at once. Take them on one at a time, and slowly your container will get bigger and bigger. As you take down your fears, more and more of what you've always wanted begins to arrive.

The enlightened perspective doesn't mean you live fearlessly, for that is all but impossible. It means you are not going to let that fear keep you from living the life you want to live.

## ✦ Sobriety

Without sobriety, you are never fully experiencing yourself or others. When under the influence of altering substances, your present-moment reality is distorted, your perception is altered, and you are not able to make real connections.

It may seem and feel like you are connected while you are under the influence—perhaps this is why some call alcohol "spirits," because you sometimes feel a spiritual connection—but once the high wears off, that warm feeling of love is gone.

Drugs and alcohol are bypasses to connection. They give you a glimpse of the experience, but it's a false experience of love, an enticing, illusionary substitute. You can get hooked on the substitute, which makes being or staying sober that much more difficult.

If you drink or use drugs, it's because you want to change the way you feel. If you felt comfortable, happy, full of love, and peaceful inside, you wouldn't have any desire to change this feeling. You didn't need drugs or alcohol to have a good time when you were a young child, so why would you need them now?

The problem is many of us don't feel comfortable, happy, and peaceful inside. We may at times not even be aware of why or what's going on inside us, just that it feels better to have that smoke, or drink, or food, or whatever it is that keeps us from feeling what is real in the moment. You may not be living the life you want to and be using something to medicate yourself to make life somewhat tolerable.

Anything you use to distract yourself from what you feel inside keeps you from growing mentally, emotionally, and spiritually.

Someone who started using alcohol or drugs regularly at the age of 16 and continues using them when feeling under stress or emotionally upset, will likely have the maturity of someone who is 16 even though he may be 55 years old.

Discomfort and pain are teachers. If you avoid experiencing these teachers, you will stay stuck. Discomfort and pain tell you where you're off track; they tell you where your perspective is separate from that of the Universe, from that of Spirit. Being unhappy, uncomfortable, and discontented are all messages telling you that you're not in alignment with what is right for you.

How about changing your life?

If you want to know where you are not right with your life, stop using alcohol or drugs or whatever it is you use to comfort yourself. Even if you are a casual, every-now-and-then user, even if you just watch TV to distract yourself, stop for a minimum of 120 days, and you'll start to experience where the rough edges of your life are.

Sobriety will show you where your heart and mind are not properly aligned with what Spirit wants for you and where you need to work on yourself.

Many people have found in their sobriety that they were with the wrong partner, in the wrong career, in the wrong city, or just in the wrong state of mind to live the life that they really want to live. Others have found great gratitude for what they have and more love in their life as a result.

The ability to maintain sobriety while working and growing through what challenging situations life can put before you is what the enlightened perspective is all about.

You must be awake to your life, able to feel it all in order to hear what the Universe is directing you to do with your life and relationships.

Being sober is synonymous with being present in the moment. In order to have healthy, loving connections, you have to be fully present. When you are sober, you are much more capable of fully being with someone because you are available mentally, emotionally, physically, and spiritually.

### ✦ Humility

The most important aspect of being humble is being able to honestly say, "I don't know" and "It's not up to me." However, your ego doesn't want to ever admit it doesn't know something or can't change something, so it will want to always produce an answer or solution in order to prove itself right, even if it doesn't really have one.

From a worldly perspective, humility is about acknowledging your shortcomings and inadequacies before others. From a spiritual perspective, it is acknowledging that the Universe is in charge and knows what it is doing. Your humility from this perspective comes from a place of knowing that there are things you don't know yet having faith that these things are as they should be.

Many situations in relationships and in life don't work the way you would like. There are many times when you are helpless to do anything to change these situations. This is when you have to surrender your will to the will of Universe and allow It to handle the situation while trusting that everything is okay as it is. Knowing what is your responsibility and what is the Universe's responsibility is an important aspect of the enlightened approach to life.

### ✦ Vision

Vision is the ability to see and understand the deeper, inner meaning of another's outer actions. Someone's outer actions may not accurately reveal what's really going on inside the person, so it's important to look for the underlying cause. A doctor who listens to your cough to determine what kind of ailment you have is an example of practicing vision. The cough is just a symptom of the underlying problem; when the underlying problem is understood, the doctor knows how to treat you.

The same goes for your relationships with others. If you've ever tried to figure out why someone did something that seemed really crazy and didn't make any sense, it's likely because he was afraid. I bet the last time you did something that was irrational or not loving or didn't make good sense, you were in a place of fear. This is true for most everyone.

For example, if your friend is upset, angry, acting out aggressively, these are all signs that he is in a fearful place, a wounded place of mind. It may be your programmed response to meet him with the same energy level he is on, with your own fear and upset. Fear affects us this way. When we're not experiencing love, we are experiencing fear; and when in fear, we can act out irrationally. Don't try to make sense of it because there is no sense to it.

However, vision is the ability to see beyond his actions to the deeper underlying experience within him. As humans, at our cores we are all pretty much the same and want the same thing—to experience the peace that comes from a loving connection. That is why it's important to look to the deeper truth behind someone's actions.

If you can see beyond the façade to the fear within, then you know he is not in his best mind. If you can't figure out why someone would do something that seems so crazy, it's likely fear; and fear doesn't make sense, so don't beat yourself up trying to understand it.

Knowing it is fear is all you need to understand. So the next time someone comes at you with hostility or something other than a loving expression, you know that he is not in his "Love-Soul Connected" mind. Even though he may not know it, you do. And you can act accordingly for how you would treat someone who is in pain or in fear.

*A Course in Miracles* teaches how someone's actions demonstrate either an inner call for love or an expression of love. Either someone is feeling empty and wanting love, or he is feeling full and sharing love. If you can break down another's actions to these two basic principles, it makes understanding others very simple.

Inner vision is also the ability to recognize and experience connection in situations where it isn't obvious. It's the ability to see the presence of Spirit and a sense of Oneness in things all around you. It's a way of viewing those around you with a loving heart and loving eyes. And it's easy to do.

This morning while I was having breakfast outside, a chickadee landed two feet away from me on my deck rail. He stopped his hurrying about for a moment, acknowledged my presence, and looked right into my eyes as if to say, "Good morning, my friend!" I looked back at him for a moment, wished him a beautiful day, and then off he flew to take care of his business.

In that moment, I experienced vision that allowed me to see past what seemed trivial, just some bird landing on my deck, to something deeper and more meaningful. I felt a sense of family, recognition, and honor between us; I felt a spiritual connection.

So when you get a call from a friend, or someone holds open a door for you, or does you a favor, or says "Hello" to you on the street, or helps you carry in the groceries, what they are really saying from somewhere inside themselves, "I see you! I love you!" You just have to know how to look for it in them, and you recognize this by looking inside yourself. Whenever you extend yourself in these ways to others, you are saying the same thing.

I suggest you try looking into the eyes of others with the mindset of "I see something divine in you, and you see it in me." Be a witness to your own experience. Try unconditionally loving everyone, even if just for today. It will change everything.

# Make Connection a Practice

*Our happiness depends on the habit of mind we cultivate,*
*so practice happy thinking every day.*
*Cultivate the merry heart, develop the happiness habit,*
*and life will become a continual feast.*

—Norman Vincent Peale

f you want to be good at something you have to practice. If you want to be great, you have to practice more. Many people, however, are very averse to doing what it is necessary to get the skills they need to be successful in relationships. They judge themselves harshly for seeking help in this area.

Loving, connected relationships are no different from anything else you want to develop. They require training and regular practice to be functional, healthy, and maturing. If you didn't know how to play the piano, you'd take lessons, right? If you didn't know how to fly an airplane, wouldn't you take lessons? You wouldn't feel ashamed of not knowing how to fly, so don't feel ashamed if you don't know how to effectively relate with others. None of us are born with good relationship skills—we have to learn them, remember them, and practice them often.

## 25 Daily Reminders for Staying Soul-Connected

1. Have faith that the Universe will lovingly take care of you.

2. Don't waste your limited time here; live and love like there is no tomorrow.

3. Consider your own feelings and the feelings of others in everything you do.

4. Don't miss an opportunity to express your love and affection for someone.

5. Avoid entanglement with self-destructive situations, behavior, and people while maintaining an open heart.

6. Become aware of your limiting fears and take action to overcome them.

7. Stay open to all possibility and accepting of change. Expect miracles to happen.

8. Be able to experience and express your full emotional range (love, fear, joy, sadness, grief, anger, etc.).

9. Respect the rights, space, time, and divinity of all creatures and one's self.

10. Honor the messages and guidance of your Inner Voice.

11. Take responsibility for your feelings, thought, and actions; don't blame others.

12. Seek the spiritual Source for love to fill you, not other people.

13. Maintain loving, truthful relationships with others.

14. Come from a place of genuine kindness and compassion; extend that to others.

15. Live in gratitude for what you have now.

16. Nurture yourself: Take time to care for your own mental, emotional, physical, and spiritual well-being.

17. Authentically be of service to others; be a giver without the need of reciprocation or acknowledgment.

18. Ask for help from others, and be open to receiving it.

19. Practice non-judgment.

20. When judgmental, forgive yourself and others.

21. Seek love and inner peace above all worldly situations or material things.

22. Maintain your self-worth independent of the opinion of others.

23. Study and know your own heart, and you will know the heart of others.

24. Remember that it's not your job to manage others, the world, or the Universe.

25. When feeling separate, love more, give more; and your life will be full.

## SEEK MORE KNOWLEDGE

When I hit my painful rock bottom, I decided I was going to commit to learning all I could.

I put aside my self-judgment about being crazy or something being wrong with me and went to see a therapist. I quickly realized that I knew very little about how to live, love, and have the inner peace I wanted; so I put together an aggressive curriculum for myself. I pieced together all I could find and created my own "relationship school."

This is what I suggest you do as well. Create a relationship school for yourself, learn all you can, and then put it into practice.

The following are some effective teaching resources you can consider when building your school and implementing your practice.

## ✦ Seminars

Individuals and international organizations hold relationship and personal growth workshops all over the world. These workshops are often held on weekends and vary from small numbers of people to hundreds attending at one time. Costs vary, but some of the best are so inexpensive that anyone can afford them. Experienced teams of therapists and relationship coaches often staff these seminars.

You can learn communication skills, interaction skills, self-management, and a whole lot about yourself you didn't know. You can also learn what it takes for you to be happy and successful in life and love.

For information about these workshops, check the Internet, ask local counselors or 12-step group attendees, or check: www.mikebiles.com.

## ✦ Counseling

Counselors are like private tutors who can train you on a one-on-one basis or in a group setting. Preferably, counselors, spiritual advisors, psychotherapists, psychologists, and life coaches have been professionally trained or have experience in facilitating.

If you don't have experience with counselors, it can be difficult to know who is good and who is wasting your time. Not all counselors are equal or necessarily right for everyone. Ask around for referrals of effective counselors, and be willing to check out a few different ones to find the right fit, the one who helps you to progress and learn. Trust your intuition. Your loyalty should be to yourself, not your counselor.

If you are being challenged, stretched, growing, and healing, you are probably with someone who is competent. A very skilled counselor can assist with improving many aspects of any relationship, at any phase. Group counseling sessions can be less expensive and sometimes are very effective as a way to learn from the lessons of others.

Many couples begin counseling as a last attempt at saving their relationship or as an effort to change their mate. I encourage counseling before entering any relationship, during a relationship, at the first signs of difficulty, and especially prior to marriage.

### ✦ Twelve-Step Groups

With beginnings in Alcoholics Anonymous, these programs have been adapted to just about every addiction, compulsion, or behavior that we can hurt ourselves with, including co-dependence, love addiction, sex, gambling, food, shopping, etc.

Participation is anonymous—in many cases you can go and sit quietly, and is by donation—so it's really affordable. And you will learn something. I attended a few meetings of every kind until I realized where I most needed to be. However, I learned something important from all of them.

If you think you might have a problem with alcohol or drugs, check out an AA meeting. If you have ever loved an alcoholic or addict, go to an Al-Anon meeting. If you have been desperate for a lover or have a sexual compulsion, attend a Sex and Love Addicts meeting. Some of these meetings may be a little difficult to find, hence the anonymity aspect. Check with counselors, social workers, churches, Internet, or hospitals for information.

## ✦ Books

Books are fantastic tools for learning, and I encourage you to read all you can. A book has been written on just about every facet of relationships.

A great way to find good books is by talking with others who've been on the growth path for a while. However, just because someone wrote a book and appears to be an expert doesn't mean that what they write about is advice you should follow. Pick the books that speak to you, make sense to you, then trust yourself with the validity of the information.

## ✦ Retreats

All kinds of retreats are out there, and some are excellent. There are yoga retreats, silent and meditation retreats, religious and spiritual retreats. There are vision quest retreats that can be up to nine days in the outdoors. There are singles and couples retreats. Most of these are held in a natural environment, away from the distractions of civilization.

Finding the right retreat may require some searching. Check alternative health magazines, bookstores, churches, postings, spiritual teachers, counselors and my website.

## ✦ Companions

Twelve-step groups have sponsors, who are like mentors and who can be very good at supporting you in your growth. Someone or a group of people on a similar path can offer you the truth from a place of caring and be supportive of your process and vice versa.

It is important to have a relationship with someone you consider a spiritual growth companion or fellow student. It's important to have someone who will hold you accountable and hold the mirror up in front of you to let you see yourself and your behavior. It may be important for this someone to not already be intimately connected or involved in your everyday life so as to be objective with their support.

### ✦ Observation

Teachers of life and love are all around you. You are presented with answers to your prayers and the lessons you need to learn every day. All you need to do is open yourself up and pay attention.

Messages you need for direction and healing can show up anywhere at any time from anyone or anything. These messages can show up in the music you listen to, the movies you watch, the books you read, or in a stranger's passing comments. Some of the biggest lessons I've learned about living a joyful life have come from watching others. Pay close attention to what is showing up in your life; it all has a lot to teach you.

### LOOKING FORWARD

Our society is in trouble. We are ill, love-starved. The symptoms are undeniable. We can no longer be healthy with the status quo way of living and loving; it's simply not working. Life and relationships are not always fun and easy; they can and will be horrendously difficult and painful at times. When they are, we just have to realize the superficial prescription for life and love we started with is not delivering or filling the hole as promised.

My hope with this book has been to open you to another way of relating, to show you that there is another way to experience love that much of the world is missing. This way is certainly not a new idea or the most popular or most understood way, but I think you'll find if you haven't already that it is far more rewarding. I encourage you to take this information, experience it for yourself in your relationships, and pass it on.

# About the Author

Mike Biles, M.A. has followed a passion for spiritual understanding and relationships since a young age. In his work, he integrates his experience with substance abuse, religion, psychology, spirituality, and martial arts. He has earned a bachelor's degree from The University of Texas School of Communications and a master's degree in Spiritual Psychology from the University of Santa Monica. He offers individual counseling, books, articles, and courses on relationship communication, spirituality, and personal development. He also offers substance abuse and behavior intervention services through a national company. For programs, information and for a free printable version of "25 Reminders for Staying Soul-Connected" visit:

www.mikebiles.com
P.O. Box 2173
Jackson, Wyoming 83001